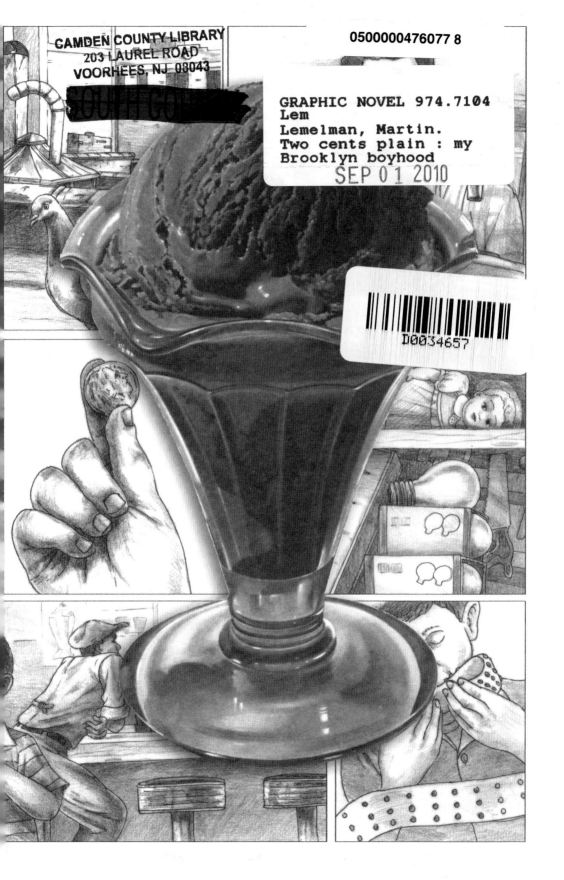

TWO CENTS PLAIN
·My Brooklyn Boyhood·

BY THE SAME AUTHOR

Mendel's Daughter

TWO CENTS PLAIN

·My Brooklyn Boyhood·

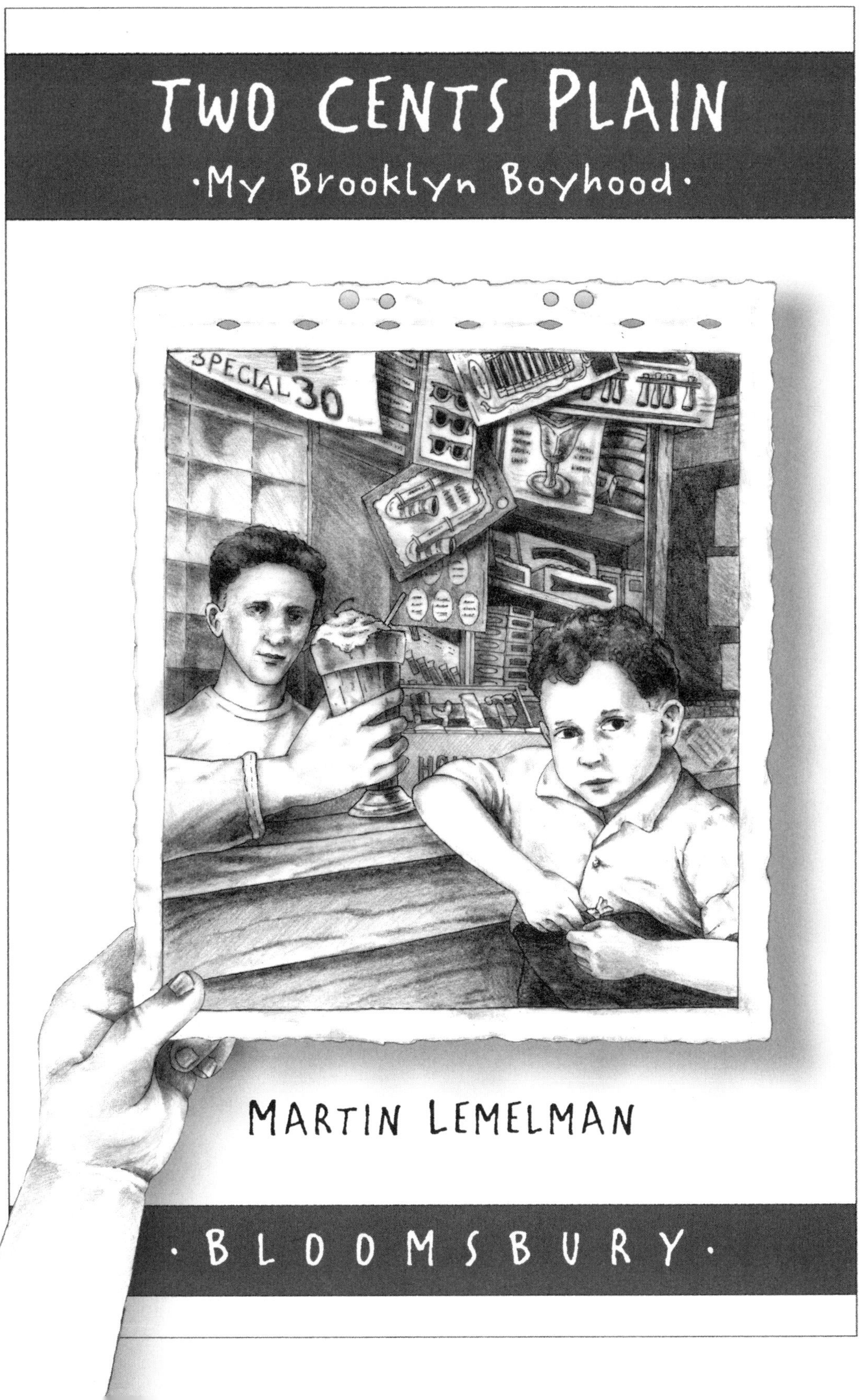
SPECIAL 30

MARTIN LEMELMAN

·BLOOMSBURY·

Published by Bloomsbury USA, New York

All papers used by Bloomsbury USA are
natural, recyclable products made from
wood grown in well-managed forests.
The manufacturing processes conform
to the environmental regulations of the
country of origin.

LIBRARY OF CONGRESS CATALOGING-IN-PUBLICATION
DATA HAS BEEN APPLIED FOR.

ISBN-978-1-60819-004-1

First U.S. edition 2010

1 3 5 7 9 10 8 6 4 2

Typeset by Westchester Book Group
Printed in the United States of America
by Worldcolor Fairfield

Days are Scrolls...

Bahya ibn Pakuda

To my brother, Bernard

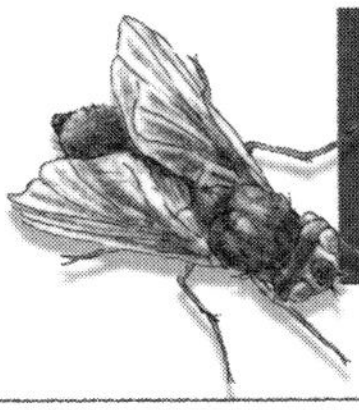

MARTIN LEMELMAN

·Mattaleh·

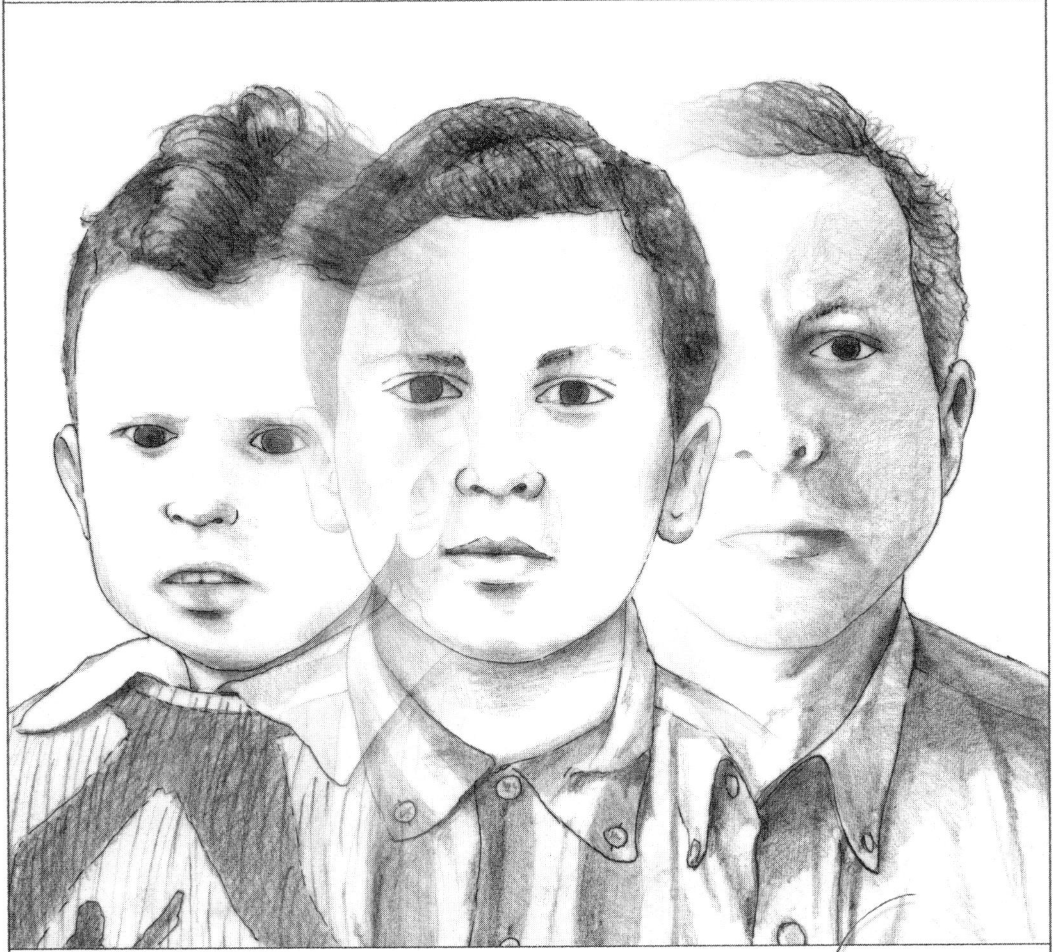

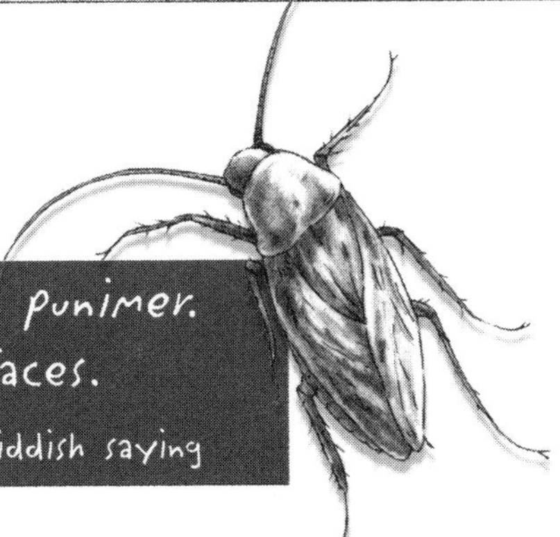

Der emmess hut asach punimer.
Truth has many faces.

Yiddish saying

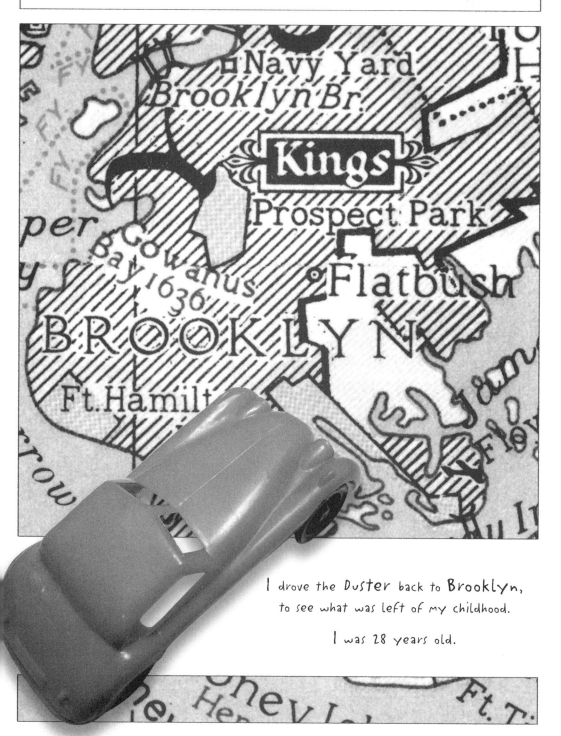

·October 1978·

It's been 10 years since we abandoned the store—
10 years since a knife was pressed to my mother's throat.

I drove the Duster back to Brooklyn,
to see what was left of my childhood.

I was 28 years old.

·BROWNSVILLE·
To get to TEDDY'S CANDY STORE, I passed
Pitkin Avenue, East New York Avenue, and Strauss Street.

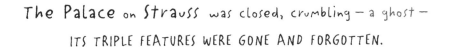
The Palace on Strauss was closed, crumbling — a ghost —
ITS TRIPLE FEATURES WERE GONE AND FORGOTTEN.

I made my way through nearly abandoned streets to Park Place and Rabbi Portnoy's Synagogue.

This was where my brother was first called up to read from the Torah scroll.

The building was still open.

It _simply_ had new tenants.

It was chilly — a typical fall day, close to my birthday.
The wind blew trash, not leaves.

448 Howard Avenue- Between Park and Prospect Place.

This is the wreck of MY father's store.

There's nothing left but the shell.

The ice cream, cigarettes, and toys have been replaced with rubble, broken glass, and splintered wood.

I SAW A BOY, *NOT ME*, WANDERING THROUGH THE RUINS.

I stopped.   Looked around.   And drove away...

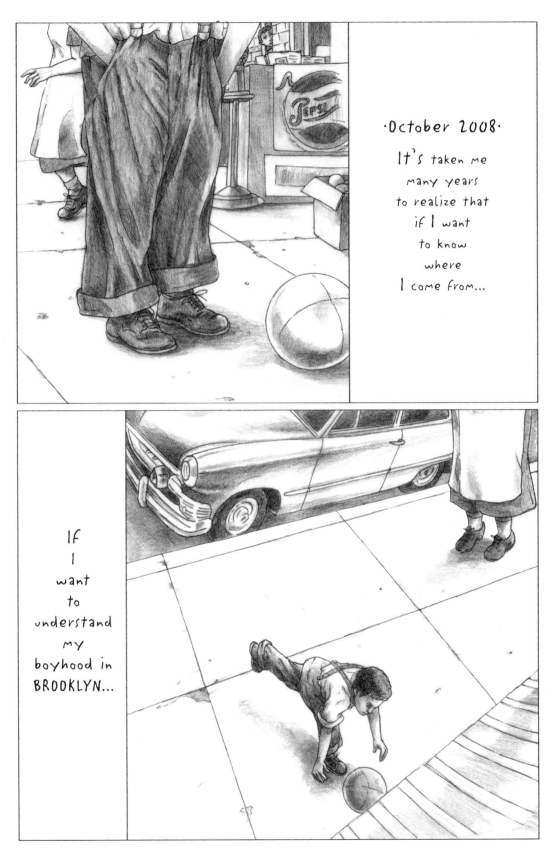

·October 2008·

It's taken me many years to realize that if I want to know where I come from...

If I want to understand my boyhood in BROOKLYN...

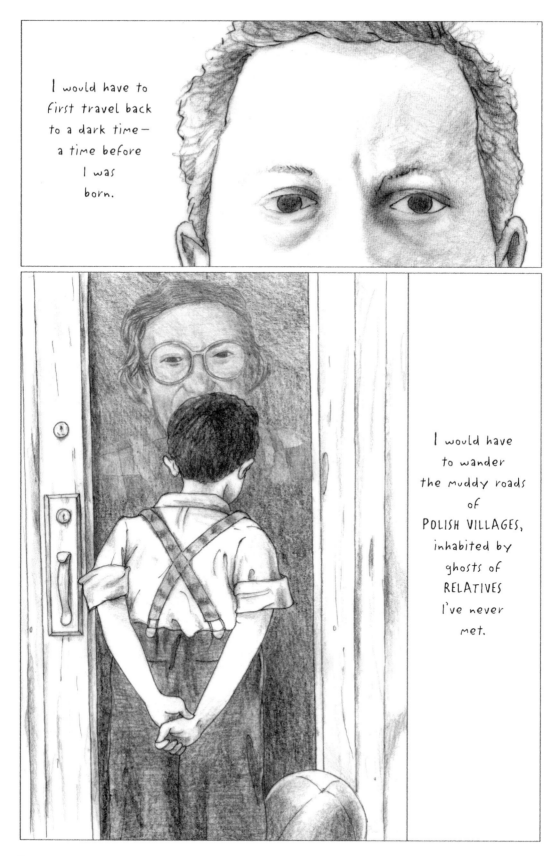

I would have to
FIRST travel back
to a dark time—
a time before
I was
born.

I would have
to wander
the muddy roads
of
POLISH VILLAGES,
inhabited by
ghosts of
RELATIVES
I've never
met.

GUSTA LEMELMAN
·My Mother's Voice·

Allis drait arum broit un toit.
Everything revolves around bread and death.

Yiddish saying

·GERMAKIVKA, POLAND·
The War came to us in 1941.

They killed your grandfather Mendel,

and your grandmother Malka,

and my little sister, Regina,

and my older sister Jenny and her husband Feivel,

and her little boy Eli.

But, I survived...

For over 2 years,
I and my brothers
Simon and Isia
and my sister
Yetala was hiding
in the Maravinitz forest—
in a hole in the ground.

This, we thought,
was going to be
OUR GRAVE.

But, in March/April 1944, the Russian Army chased out the Nazis from around our town. We believed we was saved.
BUT, STILL WE HAVE TROUBLES.

When the head Russian officer first looked on us, he said,
"How could you survive, when all the rest was killed?
YOU ARE GERMAN SPIES FOR SURE."

(In that time the Russians was shooting spies. We hear the bullets.)

I looked at this officer and in my mind I was SCREAMING, "What kind of a God are you that you should kill us after you rescue us?"

But from my mouth comes, "Sir, this is not true that we are spies.

"Listen, I will show you the grave we lived in. You will see the holes we was hiding our food— our sugar beets, our potatoes.

YOU WILL SEE THE PROOFS ON HOW WE LIVED."

Then... when he saw OUR GRAVE, when he smelled this filthy hole in the ground, his eyes opened up. He said to us, "I can't believe what I see here. I just can't believe."

But, he did believe. We was free.

My brothers joined with the Russian soldiers to fight the Germans.

And I and Yetala walked back to our town, Germakivka, in a hope to settle again in my father's house.

You should know, I found people living there.

When we was in hiding, neighbors, the MUSIKERS, wanted a better house— so they stole ours.

"You are supposed to be DEAD," Mrs. Musikers told to me. "YOU DON'T BELONG HERE NO MORE."

Oy, it wasn't enough what the Germans done. The Ukrainians and the Poles wished us in the ground, too.

Soon, we heard that they was murdering Jews— EVEN AFTER THE WAR.

It became clear that our town was no place for a Jew.

GERMAKIVKA
was for my sister
Yetala
and for me
a GRAVEYARD,
filled with
the memories of all
our dead family,
all our dead friends.

One night we just packed up.

We took some changes of clothing,
my father, **Mendel's**,
wine cup,
and my mother, **Malka's**,
needleworks,
and family pictures.

The rest we left.

In our hearts,
we knew
we was finished
with **Poland**.

We went west, to find the **American Zone**.

Late in July 1946 I and **Yetala** came to the **NEU FREIMANN DISPLACED PERSON CAMP**.

There was gates with wire and barbed wire. **American soldiers** with guns was watching over us. I was thinking, "What, did we leave one fire for another?"

"**As** matters now stand, we appear to be treating the **Jews** as the Nazis treated them except that we do not exterminate them. They are in concentration camps in large numbers under our military guard instead of S.S. troops."

Harrison Report

(Earl G. Harrison was U.S. representative on the Intergovernmental Committee on Refugees.)

"FIRST, WHEN WE REMOVE AN INDIVIDUAL GERMAN
WE PUNISH AN INDIVIDUAL GERMAN,
WHILE THE PUNISHMENT IS NOT INTENDED
FOR THE INDIVIDUAL BUT FOR THE RACE.
FURTHERMORE, IT IS AGAINST MY ANGLO-SAXON
CONSCIENCE TO REMOVE A PERSON FROM A HOUSE,
WHICH IS A PUNISHMENT, WITHOUT DUE PROCESS OF LAW.
IN THE SECOND PLACE, HARRISON AND HIS ILK
BELIEVE THAT THE DISPLACED PERSON IS A HUMAN
BEING, WHICH HE IS NOT, AND THIS APPLIES
PARTICULARLY TO THE JEWS,
WHO ARE LOWER THAN ANIMALS."

General George S. Patton

Who knew we would leave one Hitler
and find another?

But then came
General Eisenhower...

I remember when he
came to see what was in the camp.
I seen him so close, like I see you now.

After he came, our life changed —
the barbed wire disappeared.
Neu Freimann was a better place to live.

Because of this I voted for him for president.
HE WAS A MENSCH, A PERSON —
not like that animal Patton.

We settled in German workers houses — three rooms and a kitchen.
Upstairs was an attic. It was like our father's house in Germakivka.
Only here we was sharing with 2 more families.

Yetala and I was in one room.

There was water in the house.
This was for us a big luxury.

Water, oh water...

In the War,
in the forest,
it was like gold to us.

We all shared the kitchen. "Gustaleh," Yetala told to me, "You make **everything** taste so good."

I cooked with the powdered eggs, powdered milk, and the margarine they gave us.

Everything I knew what to do with, except the potato chips the **American soldiers** distributed to us.

Do I cook them? Do we eat raw?

Nobody knew.

I make from this bag a **soup**. (I also put in carrots and onions.)

THIS WAS DELICIOUS.

Who could believe, in just a few years, I would sell POTATO CHIPS in **Brooklyn, New York?**

I didn't know nothing from **America**.

The first time I saw a BLACK PERSON— a soldier in **Neu Freimann**, I was thinking maybe his skin color could wash off.

WHAT A STUPID GIRL I WAS.

Yetala and I didn't expect to see our brothers Simon and Isia again.

You can't imagine what a wonder it was when my older brother, Simon, called out to us on a street in Neu Freimann.

"YETALA, GUSTALEH," my brother Simon cried out.

In the whole Europe, he found where we was settled.

This was a MIRACLE!

"I asked all over for you," he says. "I traveled to the Pognitz DP camp, the Hedenheim DP camp, the Leipheim DP camp. I looked on lists. But, I had no luck until I came to Neu Freimann."

Simon went home with us.

We put a mattress in the kitchen for him to sleep.

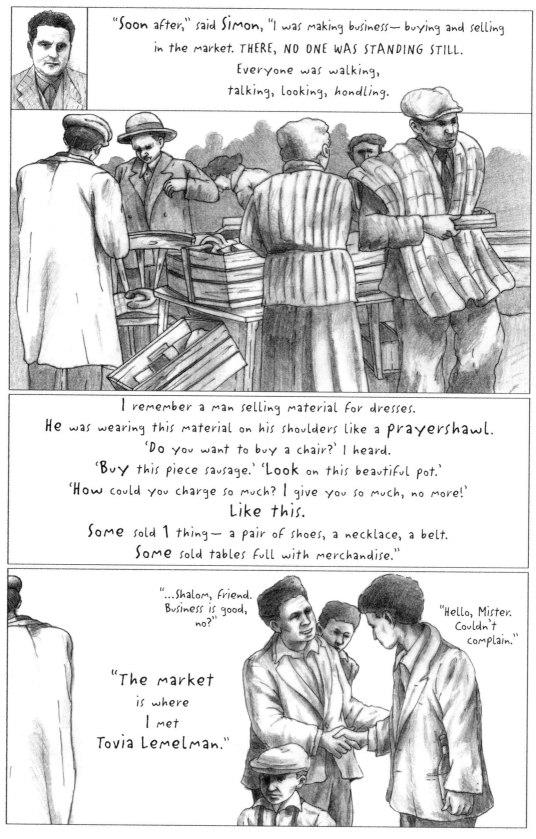

"Soon after," said Simon, "I was making business — buying and selling in the market. THERE, NO ONE WAS STANDING STILL. Everyone was walking, talking, looking, hondling.

I remember a man selling material for dresses.
He was wearing this material on his shoulders like a **prayershawl**.
'Do you want to buy a chair?' I heard.
'Buy this piece sausage.' 'Look on this beautiful pot.'
'How could you charge so much? I give you so much, no more!'
Like this.
Some sold 1 thing — a pair of shoes, a necklace, a belt.
Some sold tables full with merchandise."

"...Shalom, friend. Business is good, no?"

"Hello, Mister. Couldn't complain."

"The market is where I met Tovia Lemelman."

TOVIA LEMELMAN
·My Father's Voice·

Dos gantseh leben iz ah milchomeh.
All life is a war.

Yiddish saying

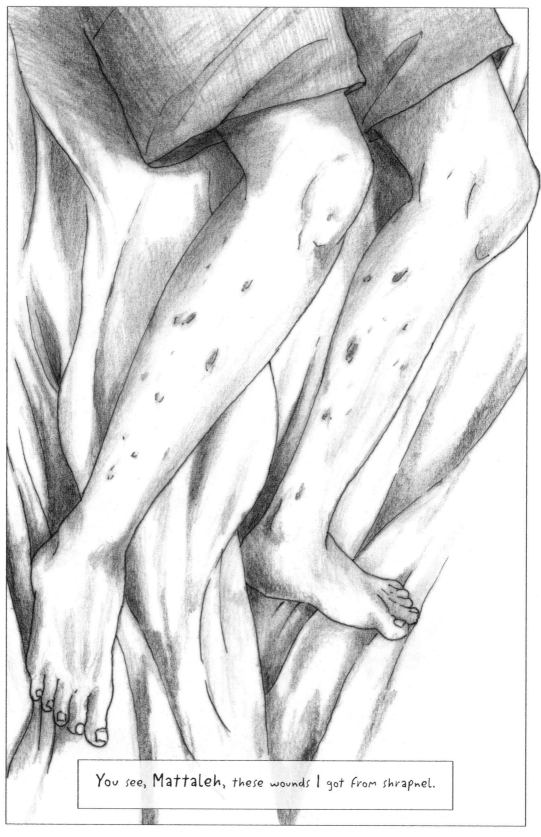

You see, Mattaleh, these wounds I got from shrapnel.

A grenade explosion ripped my legs in the **battle of Kharkov**. For 5 years I was a fighter— a sergeant in the great **Soviet Army**.

I also made the **food** for my unit.

"**Lemelman**, you make a delicious soup."

"**Tovia**, you can make a meal from nothing."

I hear this all the time.

A piece horsemeat, a sack of kasha, sometimes a chicken— I always can find something good for my comrades to eat. **My soldiers** are never hungry. All I need is a couple onions, a garlic, and I make everything delicious.

Besides this, I make **schnapps** from anything — from potatoes, even **shaving lotion**.

How, you ask? I tell you.

You put an onion in the shaving lotion and leave overnight. This **shnapps** will warm you a whole day.

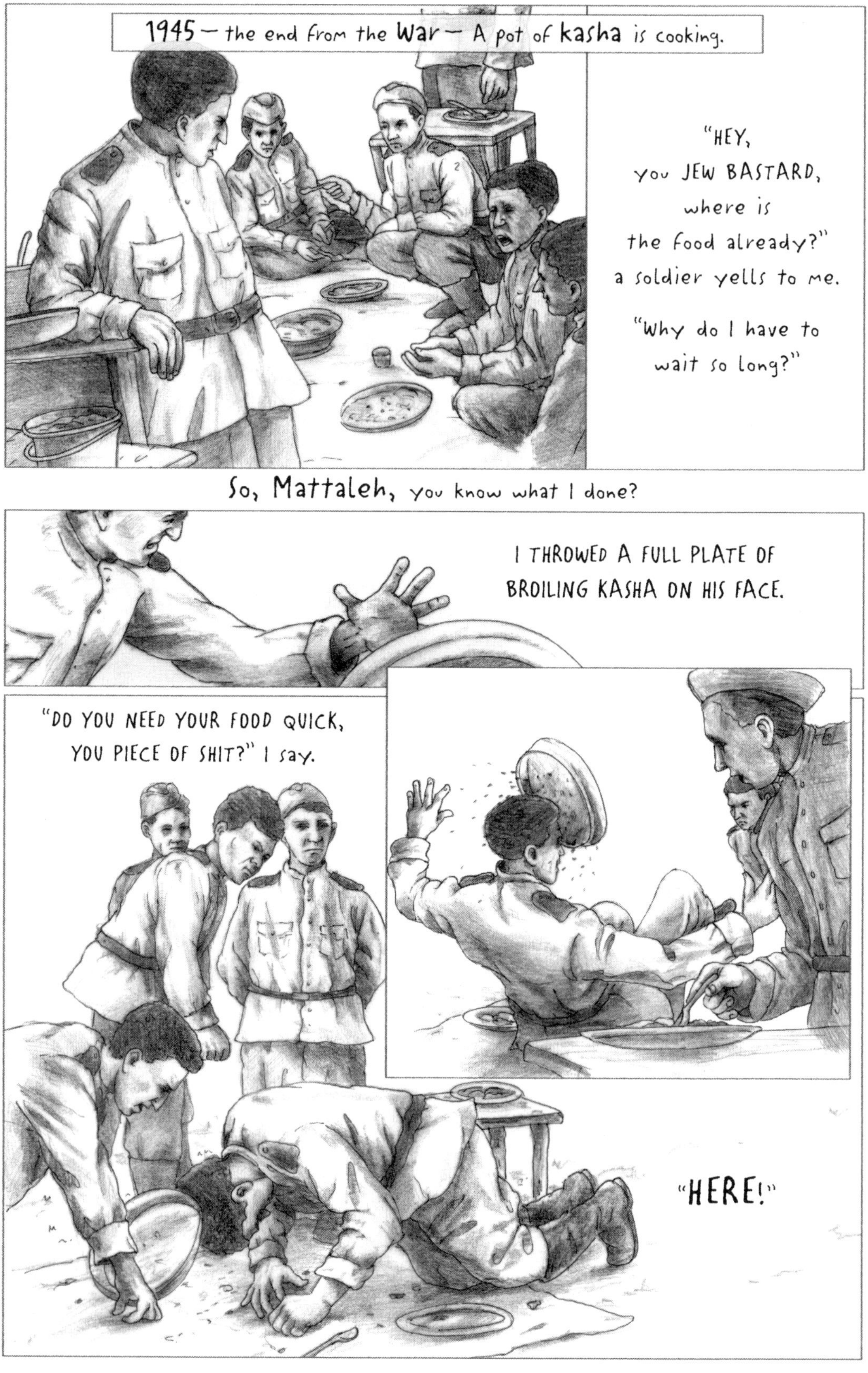
1945 – the end from the War – A pot of kasha is cooking.
"HEY, you JEW BASTARD, where is the food already?" a soldier yells to me.
"Why do I have to wait so long?"
So, Mattaleh, you know what I done?
I THROWED A FULL PLATE OF BROILING KASHA ON HIS FACE.
"DO YOU NEED YOUR FOOD QUICK, YOU PIECE OF SHIT?" I say.
"HERE!"

For this,
they arrested me
and
throwed me
in jail.

To be a
Soviet fighter
and to be called
a "Jew bastard,"
how could
this be?

I told my story
to the court,
and they
let me go.

SOON AFTER, I WROTE A LETTER.

My Dear Comrade Stalin,

I am in the army the
whole war. I fight with all
my strength for 5 years,
for you and for the
freedom of the Soviet Union.
Now please, I beg you,
to let me free. I am a Jew
and want to go home to
see what is left from
my family.

With all respect,
Tovia Lemelman

Mattaleh, you have to believe me when I tell you, Stalin answered me back. They let me go away from the army and I walked back to my town.

·RADZIWILL, POLAND·

Not one from the family did I find there.*

All the Jews was like ERASED. Even the matsayveh, the gravestone of my father, may he rest in peace, was no more.

The Gentiles took away all the stones in the Jewish cemetery— for to make roads, for who knows what...

I saw young boys playing soccer on top of the ground, where once was the gravestones.

"Are you looking for where the Jews went?" a Christian neighbor asked me.

"If you want, I will show you."

*Only later did I find out some survived.

26

We climbed a hill outside my town.

"Here the Germans shot all the Jews from Radziwill and the villages around," the neighbor man said.

"They covered the victims with dirt, and for weeks after, THIS SAME GROUND WAS MOVING AND BOILING UP."

Here and there, I found bones on the ground.

THE EARTH SPIT THEM OUT.

This I saw with MY own eyes.

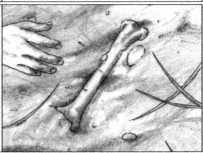

In my heart, I knew, I was finished with Poland.

I HAD ENOUGH.

I went out from Radziwill and walked west to the American Zone.

I walked and walked until I made holes in the shoes.

Finally, I came to the NEU FREIMANN DISPLACED PERSON CAMP.

IRO
AREA TEAM 1065
NEU FREIMANN
SIEDLUNG

They put me in with the bachelors.

I got a mattress, and they showed me where to sleep.

They gave me a plate, a cup, a spoon, and a fork.

IT WAS GOOD TO BE SETTLED AGAIN.

Here, Mattaleh, is the spoon and fork I used in Neu Freimann.
Feel how light they are. They made them from aluminum.

I seen some people walking around the whole day doing nothing. They didn't look like people no more.

Me— I started to make **business** in the market.

I organized schnapps, cigarettes, aspirins.

THESE I WAS BUYING AND SELLING.

This is where I met Simon.

He was selling what I was selling.

"Tovia," he says to me, "we should go into **business together.** You are good in finding the merchandise and I am **maybe better in selling.**"

"In this way we could make more **gelt.**"

"I don't need no **partner,**" I say, but I am thinking maybe he's right — maybe we could make more profit together.

I decided to take a chance.

I worked with him and, you know, **we did a good business.**

A few weeks went by, and **Simon** invited me to his house.
"**We** will drink ah glaysel tay," he says.
"First a glass tea, then we will talk."

When I came to Simon's house, I saw a beautiful young woman looking out from the window. She has black, curly hair and a pretty face.

This is the time I first put my eyes on your mother.

"When I was looking out of the window, I saw a handsome man — your father," says my mother. "Back in Neu Freimann, he still had his big white teeth. I also saw his beautiful dark green eyes.

This is the time I first looked on your father."

"Simon introduced me to his two sisters. Gusta I liked very much."

After this first visit, I came to Simon's house many more times— to talk business with him and to see Gusta.

She gave me tea with nut kichlach, cookies, and cheese blintzes.
She fed me with potato verenikas.
EVERYTHING she made was delicious!

"Gustaleh, your cooking is tam Gan Eden," I said to her. "A taste of Paradise— just like from my mother, may she REST IN PEACE."

In that time I was 36-37 years old.

I decided it was time for me
to marry and to start a family.

You know, the Torah says,
'It is not good for
a man to be alone.'

"In the beginning your father was
talking so nice, so refined," says Mommy.

"'Gustaleh, your face shines
azoy vee dem zin in Tammuz,
like the sun in July.'
LIKE THIS HE SPOKE.

Not long after we met
he asked me to
marry him.

I said 'YES.' But, even before
the words came out from my mouth,
I was thinking,
'Did I make a big mistake?'
For sure, I wanted to marry,
but I wasn't so sure your father
would be a good husband.

He was a little old.
He was wild.
HE WAS TOO NICE.

(This bracelet
he gave me in
Neu Freimann.)"

32

Our wedding was on the 25th December 1946.

Peoples was marrying every day in Neu Friemann.
WE ALL WANTED TO START A NEW LIFE. Can you blame us?

Mattaleh, you should know,
December is an important month
for the mother and me.

We married in December
and in December we passed away.

I died in 1984. She died in 1996.

33

Soon after, we was cleared for America.

In that time a ticket costs $200.00. Cheap, no?

But this price, for us, was like a million dollars. Who had this kind of money?

THE JOINT (American Joint Distribution Committee) helped us.

"Tovia, God willing, these tickets will be our escape from Europe— from this graveyard."

"Gustaleh, to have success with you is my hope."

On April 25, 1947, we left Europe.

"The whole way to America I was throwing up."

S.S. MARINE MARLIN · PORTLAND OISE·

Your mother became nauseous just smelling the mustard in the meat sandwiches they was giving us to eat. After a little time, EVERYTHING was making her sick.

"Lay down, Gustaleh, it will make you feel better."

Later, we found out she was pregnant.

A MESSAGE TO YOU FROM THE
UNITED SERVICE FOR NEW AMERICANS

א װארט צו אײך פֿון די ...

די יוניטעד סױרװיס פֿאר ...

United Service for New Americans extends its heartiest greetings to you on your arri...
of America. We are happy that we have been able to help you immigrate to this country by ...
Affidavit in your behalf. The "Joint" (American Joint Distribution Committee, our cooperating ...
presented our affidavit to the American Consul in arranging for your visa.

Now that you have arrived in the United States, we are prepared to help you furth...
shelter, our representatives will take or direct you to the hotel that has been arranged especially ...
will also help you obtain other immediate necessities.

You have completed the greatest part of your journey to a new home. C...
decide is where you will live in this country. Our staff of social workers at the hotel ...
telephone COrtlandt 7-9700) will be glad to discuss this with you. They can tell y...
United Service for New Americans can be used to help you in deciding where to ...
of your choice.

The 5,000,000 Jews of the United States are scattered throughout all par...
United Service for New Americans may help you to settle, there is a community ...
interested in helping you to build a new life for yourself in America.

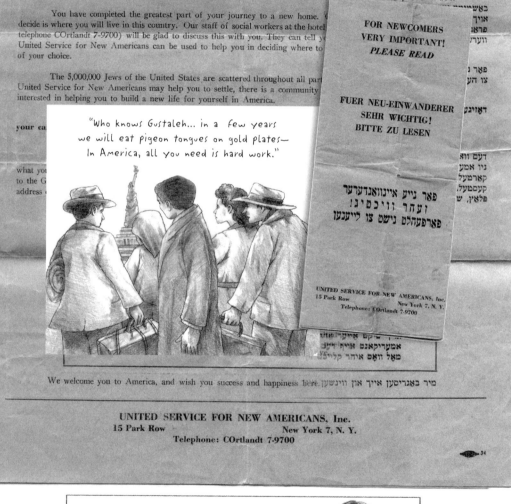

"Who knows Gustaleh... in a few years
we will eat pigeon tongues on gold plates—
In America, all you need is hard work."

FOR NEWCOMERS
VERY IMPORTANT!
PLEASE READ

FUER NEU-EINWANDERER
SEHR WICHTIG!
BITTE ZU LESEN

פֿאר נײע אײנװאנדערער
זעהר װיכטיג!
פֿארפֿעהלט נישט צו ליענען

UNITED SERVICE FOR NEW AMERICANS, Inc.
15 Park Row   New York 7, N. Y.
Telephone: COrtlandt 7-9700

We welcome you to America, and wish you success and happiness here. מיר באגריסען אײך און װינשען ...

UNITED SERVICE FOR NEW AMERICANS, Inc.
15 Park Row   New York 7, N. Y.
Telephone: COrtlandt 7-9700

"Pigeon tongues I didn't want.
To be rich was not for me.
TO LIVE A NORMAL LIFE WAS MY DREAM."

THE AMERICAN SURPRISE

NO. 96

SCHOOL CRAYONS
9 COLORS

Afflicted one, storm-tossed, and not comforted— See, I will set your stones in fair colors, and lay your foundations with sapphires.

Isaiah 54:11

I gave birth to
your brother, Bernard,
on the 6th December 1947.

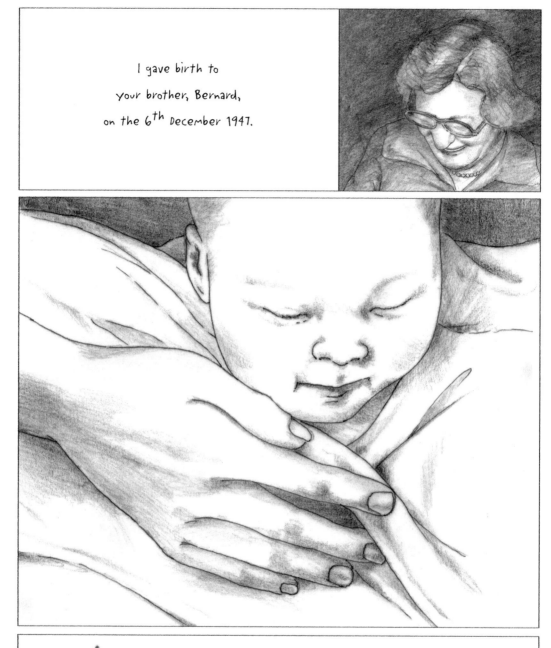

HE WAS THE FIRST AMERICAN CITIZEN IN OUR FAMILY.

I was so happy, but you know, I cried too.

My mother, Malka, and my father, Mendel,
may they rest in peace,
didn't live to see my beautiful boy.

In this time, we rented rooms in a tenement—78 Clinton Street.
Your brother grew his first 2-3 years here.

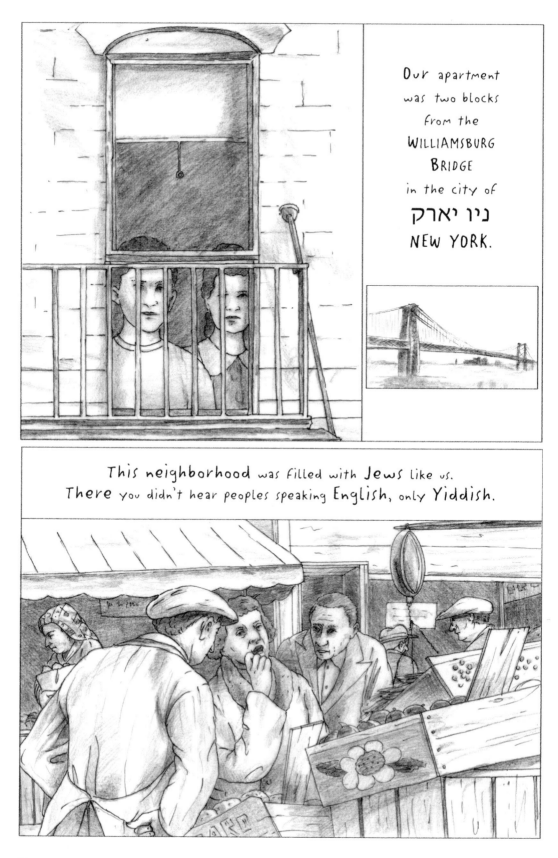

Our apartment was two blocks from the **WILLIAMSBURG BRIDGE** in the city of ניו יארק NEW YORK.

This neighborhood was filled with **Jews** like us. There you didn't hear peoples speaking **English**, only **Yiddish**.

"My first job in the UNITED STATES," deh Tateh says, "was in a kosher delicatessen.

A Jew, an American citizen gave me work to wash dishes."

For this kind of job you didn't need to speak no English.

"What kind of a name is Tovia?" the owner says to me in Yiddish. "Bah, this is a greenhorn name. You want to work for me, you need a good American name."

This is how I got the name TEDDY.

I never went back after the first day. "Did I come to the United States to wash dishes?" I asked myself. The owner never paid me for my work. So the only thing I got from this job was my new American name, Teddy.

After this, I wandered around the neighborhood looking for work.

10 blocks from our rooms, I found a Candy Store. The address was number 640 East 5th Street.

"I am good with buying and selling," I said to myself. "MAYBE *THIS* IS FOR ME."

So the owner and me signed a two year lease for $30 a month.

He sold us the fountain, the carbonator, and all the the merchandise for $1,270.00 — a good price, I think."

You should know that even before we opened up, we was makin' money!

The ladies from the building paid $2.00 a month to leave the baby carriages in the back from the store.

They didn't want to schlep the heavy carriages up the steps.

AH, AMERICA... *LEYBEN ZOL COLUMBUS, LONG LIVE COLUMBUS!*

The man teached me how to use the fountain... He show me how to make an EGG CREAM, how to scoop the ICE CREAM, to make a FRAPPE, an ICE CREAM SODA, a MALTED — everything.

"Tovia," he told to me, "You need to know the difference between Coca-Cola and Pepsi-Cola. The peoples will be angry if you make a mistake from this."

(He was right, Mattaleh. I tell you, peoples are crazy. It's the same drek.)

"The man showed me how to order, what to order, when to order," says Mommy. "Me, now that we have a store, I have to learn to talk English, to write English.

Your father, the stubborn akshin— he was not interested in this. He already learned everything he needed to know in Europe, he told me."

"Did I want this store? More no than yes."

But, how else can I support THE FAMILY?

In POLAND I had fields. I managed a mill. People was treating me with respect.

What did I have here?

Nothing... A Candy Store.

From AMERICA, I wanted better.

·CHICKEN FARM·

Youngsville, N. Y.

Krich nisht tzu hoich, vestu nisht darfen falen.
Don't climb too high and you won't have to fall.

Yiddish saying

46

A few months went by...
In the store I was hearing that some Jews, greenhorns like us, was leaving the neighborhood and settling on chicken farms.

I liked this idea...

"Nu Isia, come, we'll have coffee. We'll talk business."

I TOLD MY BROTHER-IN-LAW MY PLAN TO BUY A FARM. MAYBE HE WOULD BE A PARTNER TO ME?

"Tovia, thanks but no thanks. I got a good job. I got money in the bank. What more do I need?"

In this time, Isia was working in a factory, sewing raincoats for the U.S. Navy.

Was in the time from the Korean War.

His paycheck was $125.00 a week— good money for 1950.

"OK boys, let's keep up the pace."

"So this makes you happy?" I said to him.
"Workin' day in, day out for a BOSS?
Makin' money for some RICH GEVIR?

WHO SAID YOU CAN'T BE RICH
AND BE YOUR OWN BOSS?"

"Tovia," he said,
"how can I give up
MY GOOD, SECURE JOB?"

PIES

"Security?" I said to him,
"this is what you want?
Didn't you learn nothing
from the War.
YOU LIVE, YOU DIE.
There's no security.
COME, TAKE A CHANCE
WITH ME."

HE DID.

Soon Isia, his wife, Jenny, I and our family moved to a farm in Youngsville.

There we have 3,000 chickens and cows, too!

To learn to be a farmer wasn't hard.

Each day we was doing the same thing.

First we waked up early.

Then we milked the cows and fed the chickens.

Sometime I took the eggs. Sometime Isia.

Day in, day out,

we did all these things.

I do remember there were little chicks
all over the place.

I was about 3 when
we lived on the farm.

I don't remember much.

I'll never forget when
a chicken
snuck into our house
and started
running across my bed.

IT SHIT ALL OVER IT!

50

"**We** didn't stay long on **the farm**," says **Mommy**. "I don't like it so much. You don't see too many peoples. And I wanted **my children** to have a Jewish education.

Youngsville was not like in **New York**..."

"**All** of a sudden, **we** wasn't making enough money," says my **Uncle Isia**.

"There was too many farmers and the prices was going down. You know, it costs so much and so much to feed the chickens and the cows.

"**We** didn't have from what to buy the food.

"**We** made some money selling our milk to a **Breakstone plant**.

But after awhile, even this plant closed down."

"I know we have big troubles," says **Daddy**. "But, if we stay, we could make a living. This I believe, with a full heart."

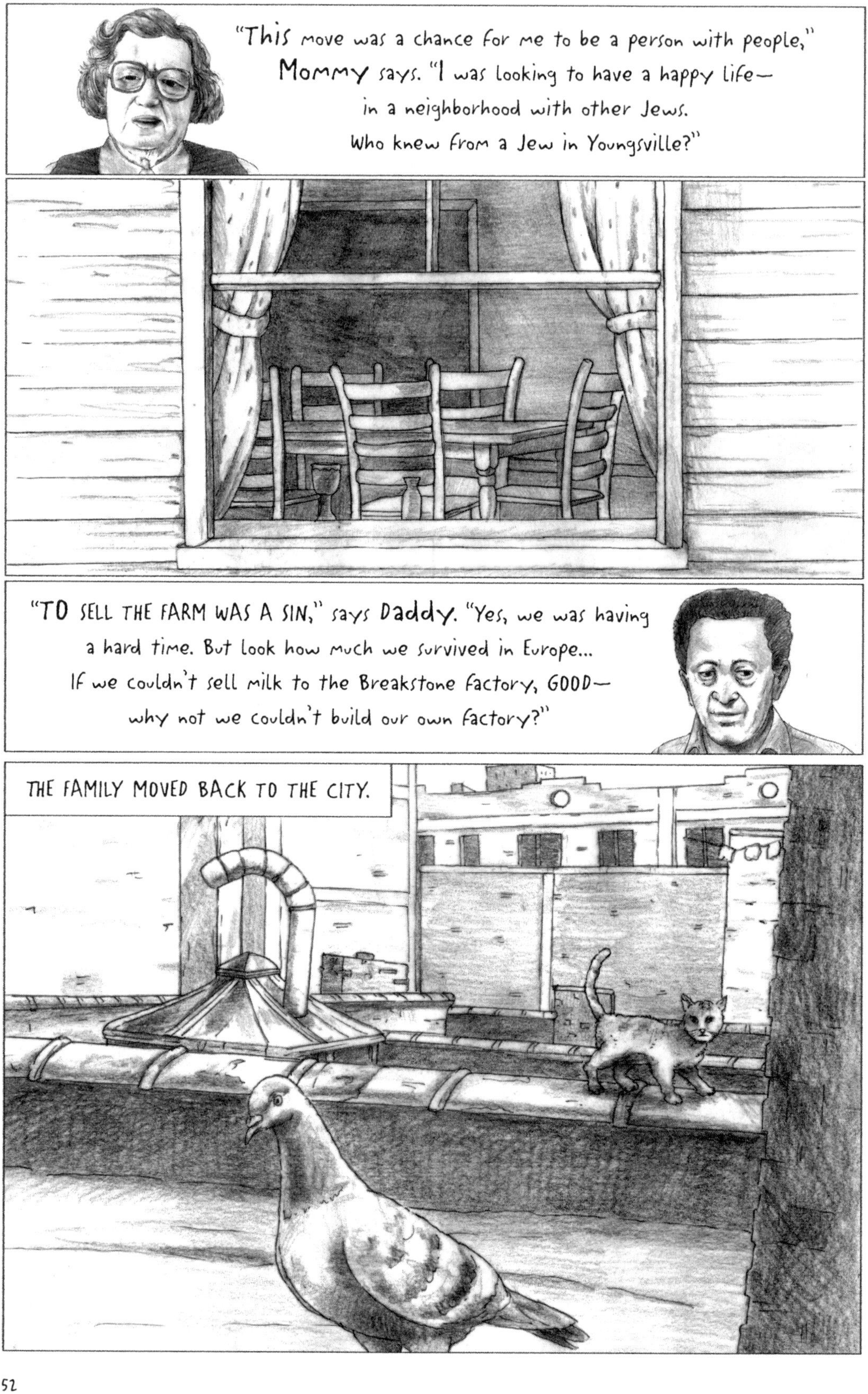
"This move was a chance for me to be a person with people," Mommy says. "I was looking to have a happy life—in a neighborhood with other Jews. Who knew from a Jew in Youngsville?"
"TO SELL THE FARM WAS A SIN," says Daddy. "Yes, we was having a hard time. But look how much we survived in Europe... If we couldn't sell milk to the Breakstone factory, GOOD—why not we couldn't build our own factory?"
THE FAMILY MOVED BACK TO THE CITY.

· THE FAMILY ·

Der leben iz di gresteh metsieh. Meh krigt es umzist.
Life is the biggest bargain. You get it for free.

Yiddish saying

This is
Mommy—
deh Mameh,
and
Daddy—
deh Tateh.

In another life
they were
known as
Gusta
and
Tovia.

NOW, IN AMERICA, PEOPLE CALL THEM GOLDIE AND TEDDY.

When I ask Mommy about her other life,
she says, "FEH, WHO NEEDS TO KNOW THIS TERRIBLE STORY."
She's set in the present— in our day-to-day existence.

When I ask Daddy about his other life,
he shows me his shrapnel-scarred legs
and tells me war stories.

This is Bernard and deh Mameh, before I entered the picture.

"Mommy and Daddy call me Boynat," says my brother. "That's how they pronounce Bernard.

If they're in a really good mood, I'm Boynishu.

"My official Yiddish names are Berel and Barrish, after my father's father. My Hebrew name is Dov. In school, some kids called me Barrel Lemonchoke."

To me, my brother is Bernie or Bernard.

ME
(Mattaleh)

I'M THE YOUNGEST
IN THE FAMILY.

I was named after Malkah,
my mother's mother.

My parents call me Mattaleh.

People in the neighborhood
call me Muttle.

My brother calls me Martin,
or sometimes, Idiot.

In school I was given the Hebrew name,
Mordechai.
Some classmates call me Mud—
others, simply Lemelman.

A nurse at the hospital helped pick my English name.
"You could name your baby, Marvin,"
she told Mommy, "or Martin or Melvin.
They all have the MMM sound, just like
your mother's name."

OY, THANK GOD,
I DIDN'T END UP
MELVIN.

·October 26, 1950, 7:05 pm·

"This was the day you was BORN.
You were, for me, a wonder..."

But soon, the happiness was cut from me.
Oy, Mattaleh, you don't know what it was like
in that hospital. I want to nurse you
and they don't let! I don't understand—
why they don't let me give you the breast?

For three days I didn't see you.
Who knows what is with you?
Chas V'shalom, heaven forbid,
maybe you is sick?

Not until I make such
a geshrai, such a yelling—
only then the nurses let me
have YOU.

They was Hitlers. How they can do this to a mother?

So then finally, after the 3rd day, they let me have you, **Mattaleh**.

They let me nurse you.

THIS MADE ME SO HAPPY.

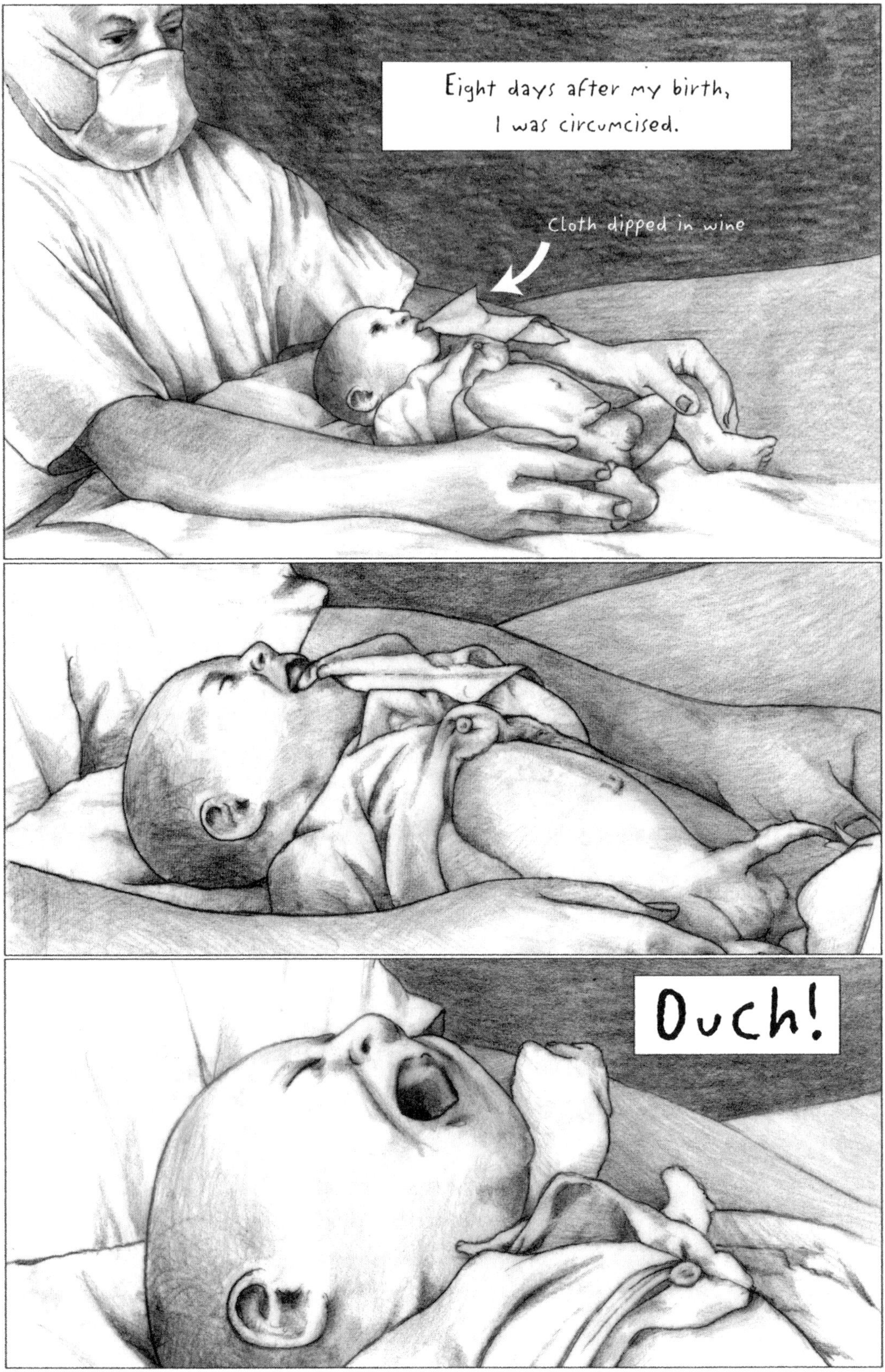
Eight days after my birth,
I was circumcised.
Cloth dipped in wine
Ouch!

"At your *bris*, I was crying more than you was crying," **Mommy** says. "You was such a little baby.

But, really, **Mattaleh**, from the minute you was born, you made me cry my eyes out.

You didn't have no **luck**. You don't have no **mazel**.

ALWAYS YOU WAS GETTING HURT OR INTO TROUBLE.

"**Did** you know, that the first thing your brother, **Boynat**, done after I bring you home from the hospital was to throw a shoe at **you**? Can you believe it?"

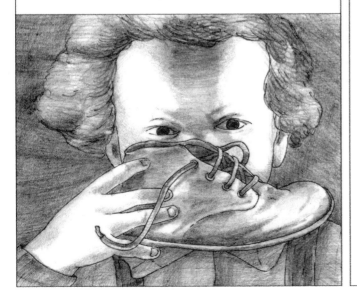

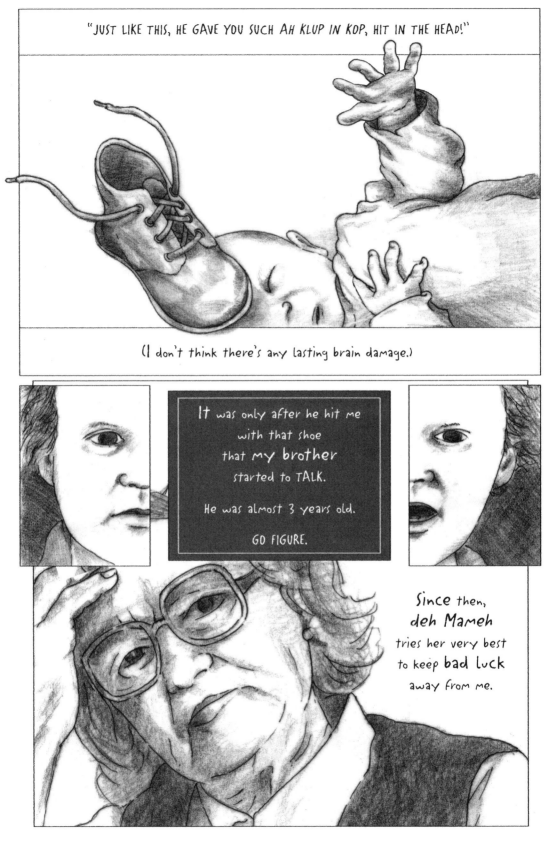

"JUST LIKE THIS, HE GAVE YOU SUCH *AH KLUP IN KOP, HIT IN THE HEAD!*"

(I don't think there's any lasting brain damage.)

It was only after he hit me
with that shoe
that MY brother
started to TALK.

He was almost 3 years old.

GO FIGURE.

Since then,
deh Mameh
tries her very best
to keep **bad luck**
away from me.

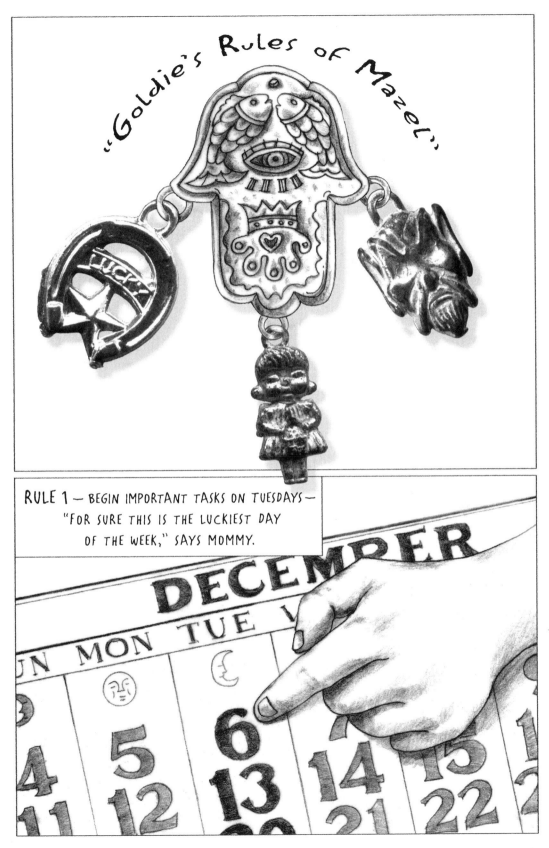

"Goldie's Rules of Mazel"

RULE 1 — BEGIN IMPORTANT TASKS ON TUESDAYS —
"FOR SURE THIS IS THE LUCKIEST DAY
OF THE WEEK," SAYS MOMMY.

RULE 2 — TUCKING A TORAH INTO BABY'S CRIB AND WRAPPING A RED RIBBON 'ROUND THE WRIST WILL PROTECT BABY FROM *AH N'HORAH*, THE EVIL EYE.

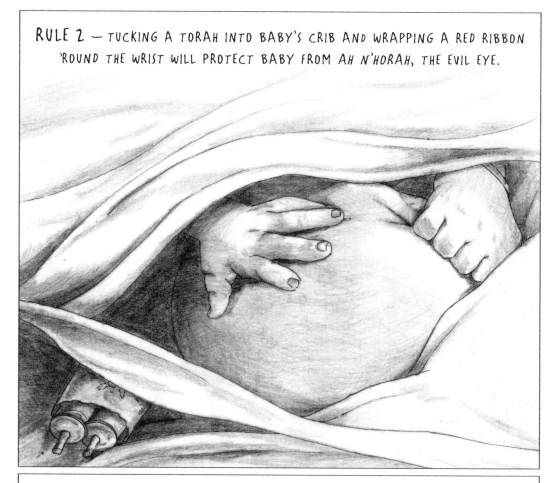

RULE 3 — AVOID HAIRCUTS BEFORE THE AGE OF THREE.
LONG HAIR ON LITTLE BOYS DUPES DEVILS, SPIRITS AND IMPS INTO MISTAKING
LITTLE BOYS FOR LITTLE GIRLS.

(And we all know imps don't give a crap about little girls.)

RULE 4 —

STEER CLEAR OF STEPPING
OVER THE LEGS OF YOUR LAD.

IT STUNTS GROWTH.

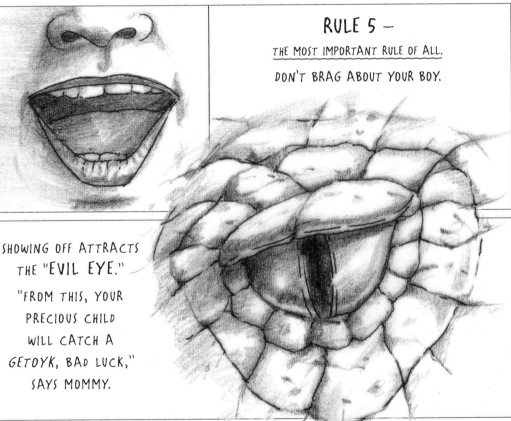

RULE 5 —

THE MOST IMPORTANT RULE OF ALL.

DON'T BRAG ABOUT YOUR BOY.

SHOWING OFF ATTRACTS
THE "EVIL EYE."

"FROM THIS, YOUR
PRECIOUS CHILD
WILL CATCH A
GETOYK, BAD LUCK,"
SAYS MOMMY.

Skeptical as I am of *GOLDIE'S RULES OF MAZEL,*
I still can't bring myself to step over the legs of my kids.
I want them to grow to their full height. (Hey, it can't hurt. RIGHT?)

·IN BROOKLYN·

BROOKLYN AND WILLIAMSBURG BRIDGES, NEW YORK CITY   20

Brooklyn Bridge at Night, New York City

PLANTERS

Tzum glik, tzum Shlimazel!
For better, for worse.

Yiddish saying

In the fall of 1951 we moved to
448 Howard Avenue,

in Brownsville,

BROOKLYN.

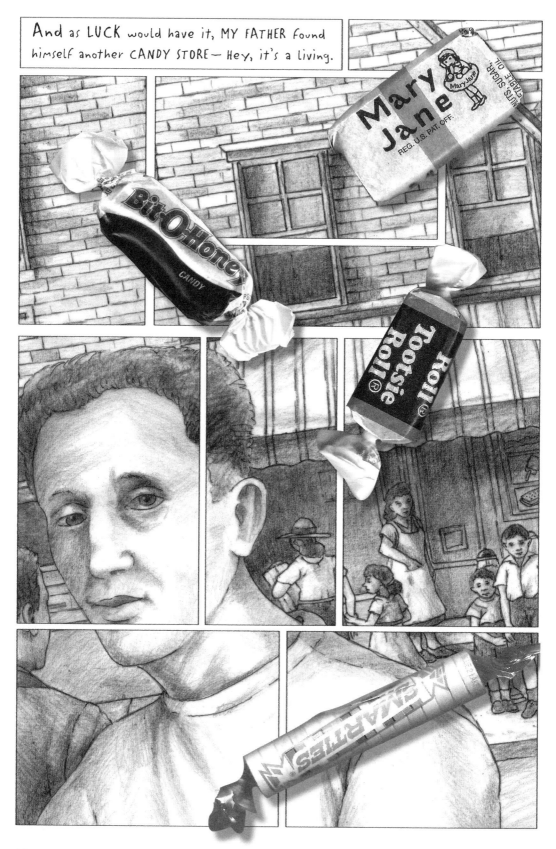

And as LUCK would have it, MY FATHER found himself another CANDY STORE— Hey, it's a living.

SNAPSHOTS of TEDDY'S CANDY STORE

The FOUNTAIN

CRATES and CAT.

PEPSI

Shelves filled with TOYS, GAMES, CIGARETTES and CANDY.

The TELEPHONE BOOTH— 10¢ a call. Our number is PResident 3-9010.

The COKE ICE BOX— FRESH ICE, delivered once a week.

The WALL of COMICS

THE STORE was crammed with "STUFF."

People came to Teddy's from as far away as Eastern Parkway (4 blocks). They'd make the trek past lots of tenements, Horn's Bakery (great rye bread—lousy cakes), and my friend Jan's house.

Jan was rich. He lived in the only single family house on the block.

If you peeked into his yard, you'd see a cement bird bath. The pigeons stopped there for drinks.

When I wasn't too busy working in the store, I played Cowboys and Indians with Jan. He had a TV way before us!

"I like going to your Daddy's store," said Jan. "For 15 cents I get a big scoop of vanilla, squashed between 2 giant oatmeal cookies."

TRUST ME— IT WAS THE BEST ICE CREAM EVER.

Lots of customers came in after shopping at the **Prospect Place Market**.

A COOL DRINK SURE HIT THE SPOT.

This lady is on her way. But first, she'll have to pass the Pharmacy on the corner.

The Pharmacy at Howard and Prospect was run by 2 partners— they looked just like LAUREL and HARDY. I AM NOT KIDDING.

"Mr. Hardy" was always fond of saying that, "An egg cream from Teddy's is to die for."

Yes, the old people liked egg creams a lot.

MR. LAUREL and MR. HARDY never found out that Daddy sold aspirin for cheaper. Shhh... It's a secret.

The Hardware and Notions store was just past the Pharmacy.

If you happened to need a lightbulb,
you didn't have to stop at the Hardware store.
You could buy one from us and get an ice cream soda.
(Daddy sold lots of items you wouldn't find in any other candy store.)

Not many people
came by car.
But, the few who did
were made to feel welcome.

As long as they brought
CASH.

"Mattaleh, Mattaleh,
why you have to talk so rough?"
deh Mameh says.

"We worked so hard to make
a living, and you have to make fun?

"The people liked our store.
We was carrying
cigarettes, candy, toys,
ice cream— everything.

"Whatever peoples was wanting to buy,
WE SELL.
Even you like all these,
or why, after so many years, you
still save all the Halloween masks,
the sunglasses, the games, the toys?"

"What schoira we didn't put out to sell," Mommy says, "went in the back, where we lived."

My Baba Malkah's surviving needlepoints. They're beautiful.

All those merchandise-filled cardboard boxes became part of our **furniture.**

My brother, Bernard, and I sat on them and played on them.

Even 50 years later, the smell of a cardboard box still takes me back to 448 HOWARD AVENUE...

OF COURSE, JUST 3 ROOMS WITH 4 PEOPLE LED TO ODD SLEEPING ARRANGEMENTS.

"I put Boynat's bed next to the refrigerator," Daddy says.

Oh, how I envied my brother.

He slept in his own room— THE KITCHEN.

"Wow, yeah, lucky me! All night long I hear the REFRIGERATOR going on, the REFRIGERATOR shutting off, the REFRIGERATOR ting off, the REFRIGERATOR going on, the REFRIGERATOR on, the REFRIGERATOR shutting off, the REFRIGERATOR off, the REFRIGERATOR going on, the REFRIGERATOR n, the REFRIGERATOR shutting off, the REFRIGERATOR off, the REFRIGERATOR going on, the REFRIGERATOR...

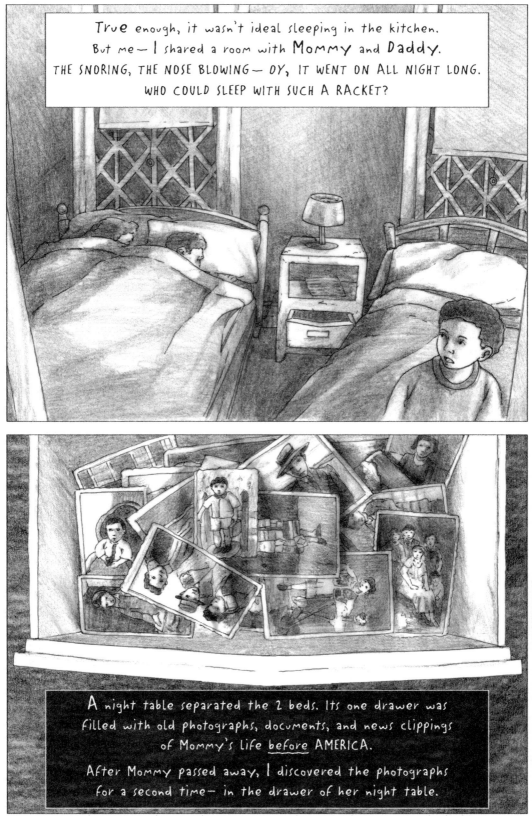

True enough, it wasn't ideal sleeping in the kitchen.
But me— I shared a room with Mommy and Daddy.
THE SNORING, THE NOSE BLOWING— OY, IT WENT ON ALL NIGHT LONG.
WHO COULD SLEEP WITH SUCH A RACKET?

A night table separated the 2 beds. Its one drawer was filled with old photographs, documents, and news clippings of Mommy's life before AMERICA.

After Mommy passed away, I discovered the photographs for a second time— in the drawer of her night table.

The night table is now in my art studio. The pictures remain inside.

· COMRADES ·

S'iz schver tzu machen ah layben.
It's hard to make a living.

Yiddish saying

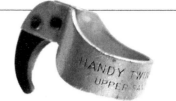

FIRST CHORE OF THE DAY

Early morning was
paper delivery time.
Newspapers,
tightly bundled with twine,
were dropped at the curb.

The street—
still dark, quiet,
asleep...

"Don't forget, **Mattaleh,**
I, too, waked up early
every morning," says **Mommy.**

"Who has to make the returns,
pay the bills, clean the floor,
and put together
the magazine and comics
for the newspapers?"

We sold the TIMES, the DAILY NEWS, the HERALD TRIBUNE, the NY MIRROR, the NY POST, the *FORVITZ*, the *MORGEN JOURNAL* the *LA PRENSA*, the *EL DIARIO*, the AMSTERDAM NEWS, the...

THE 1950's was a time for MANY NEWSPAPERS...

My job was to stand outside and collect the pennies, nickels, and dimes from customers who were in a hurry. "Sorry, only the paper today," they'd say. I'm known as "MATTALEH, THE EXPRESS SERVICE."

It was outside of Teddy's that I learned to make change.

One of the benefits of owning a CANDY STORE was being able to look at the SUNDAY COMICS BEFORE ANYONE ELSE.

THE SUNDAY PAPERS were made up of many, many parts—
THEY WERE ENORMOUS.
The comics, the ads, and the magazine sections
were delivered early in the week.

Then retailers like us sandwiched these sections with
the news delivered on Saturday night and Sunday morning.

I HELPED WITH THIS JOB, TOO.

The customers began to trickle in around 6.

"This is when I have ah glaysel kava," Daddy says. "A glass from coffee."

He drank standing up, behind the counter.

Fact is, my father didn't need much FOOD.

He survived on gallon after gallon of black, unsweetened COFFEE.

Also, he couldn't do without CIGARETTES.

The first customers to arrive were
his COMRADES, the LANDSLEIT.
These men worked in the neighborhood.
Teddy's was their quick break before they began their busy days.
Like us, they were people starting over...

"DER DELI MAHN"
smelled of salami—
not necessarily
an unpleasant odor.

"Ah gut morgen, Tovia.
Please, for me,
a glass seltzer water—
a two cents plain."

A few times a year, Mommy took Bernard and me to his delicatessen
for a potato knish and a hot dog. And even if the store was only across the street
and down the block, I really looked forward to "going out to eat."

"Mattaleh, we don't have time to eat out today.
Maybe you would like a hot dog to take home, instead?"

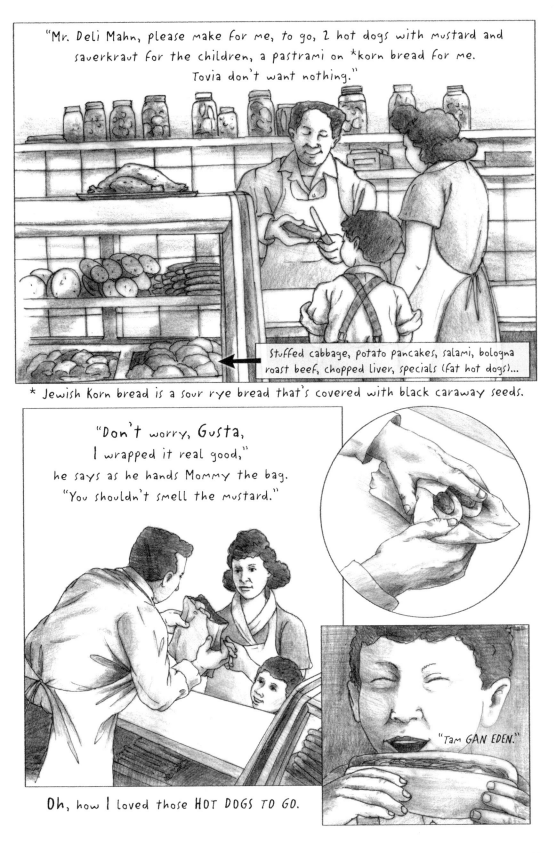

"Mr. Deli Mahn, please make for me, to go, 2 hot dogs with mustard and sauerkraut for the children, a pastrami on *korn bread for me. Tovia don't want nothing."

Stuffed cabbage, potato pancakes, salami, bologna roast beef, chopped liver, specials (fat hot dogs)...

* Jewish Korn bread is a sour rye bread that's covered with black caraway seeds.

"Don't worry, Gusta, I wrapped it real good," he says as he hands Mommy the bag. "You shouldn't smell the mustard."

"Tam GAN EDEN."

Oh, how I loved those HOT DOGS TO GO.

"Just the FORVITZ for me today, Tovia."

דער פיש מאן

"DER FISCH MAHN"
Even before
he opened his store,
Manny stank of fish.
His apron
was always dirty.

I BET HE WAS BURIED SMELLING OF FISH.
But, you know what...
He always had a smile on his face.

IF you walked past
his store,
you couldn't miss the live carp
swimming right there
in the window.

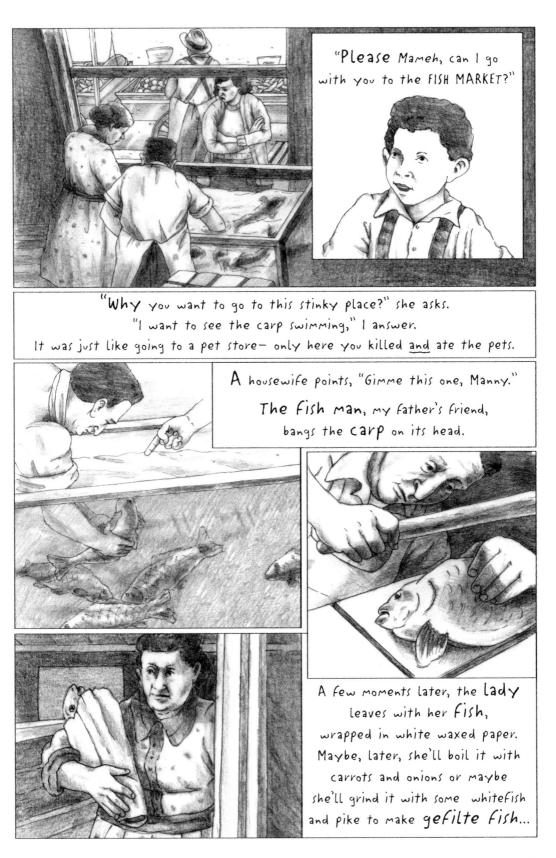

"Please Mameh, can I go with you to the FISH MARKET?"

"Why you want to go to this stinky place?" she asks.
"I want to see the carp swimming," I answer.
It was just like going to a pet store— only here you killed and ate the pets.

A housewife points, "Gimme this one, Manny."

The fish man, my father's friend, bangs the carp on its head.

A few moments later, the lady leaves with her fish, wrapped in white waxed paper. Maybe, later, she'll boil it with carrots and onions or maybe she'll grind it with some whitefish and pike to make gefilte fish...

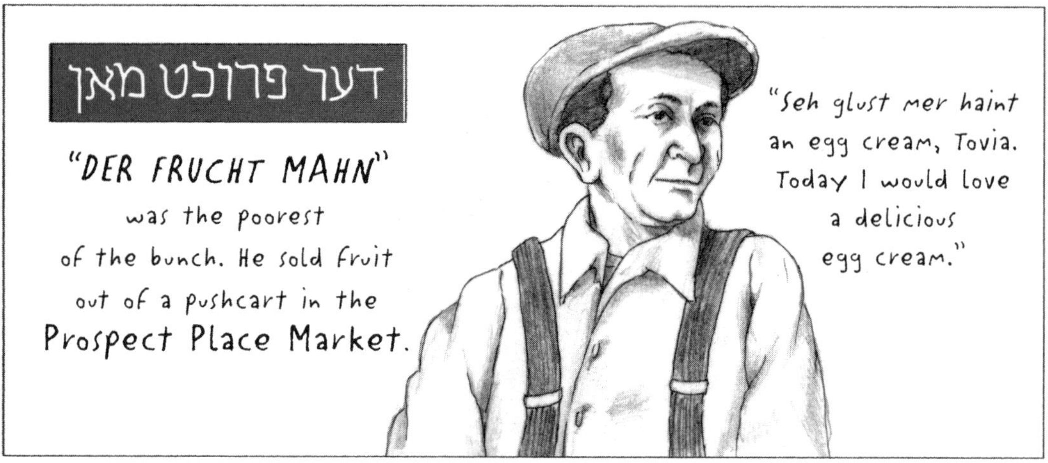
דער פרוכט מאן
"DER FRUCHT MAHN"
was the poorest of the bunch. He sold fruit out of a pushcart in the Prospect Place Market.
"Seh glust mer haint an egg cream, Tovia. Today I would love a delicious egg cream."

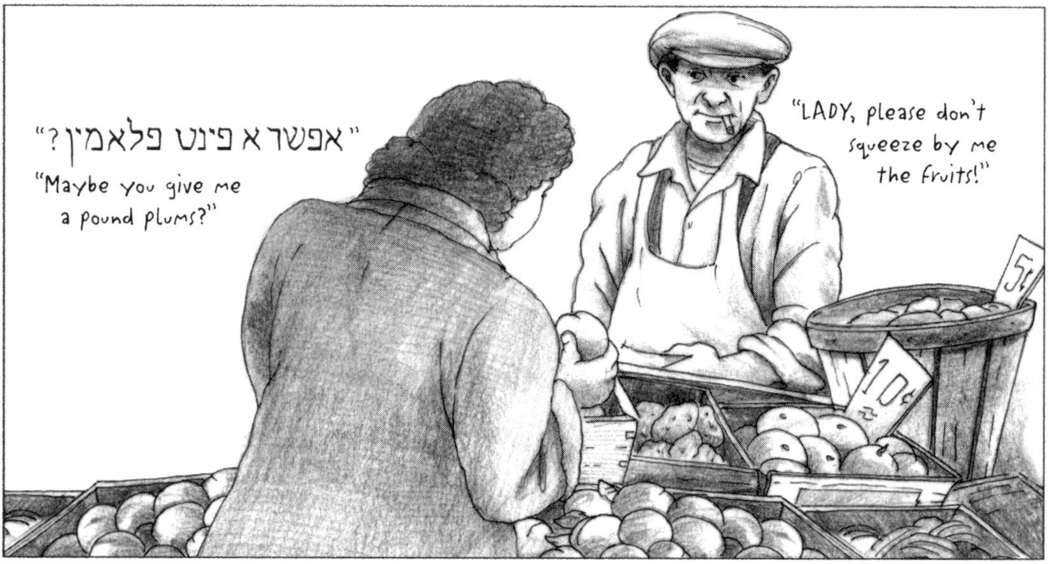
"אפשר א פינט פלאמין?"
"Maybe you give me a pound plums?"
"LADY, please don't squeeze by me the fruits!"
5¢
10¢

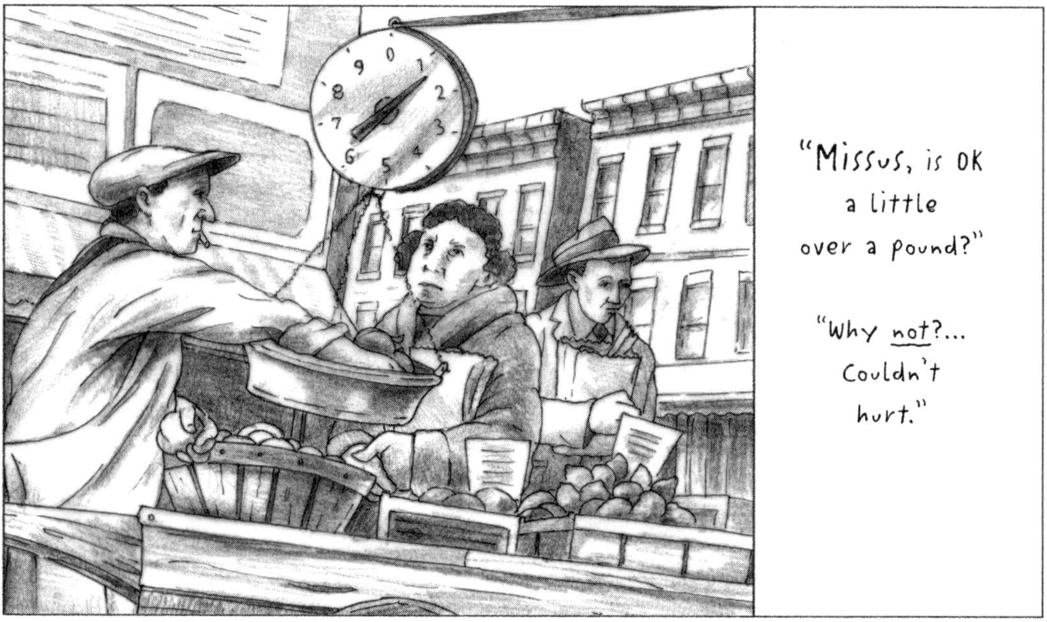
"Missus, is OK a little over a pound?"
"Why not?... Couldn't hurt."

"So one of his landsleit asked the another, 'How's business?'" Mommy says.
"Another answered, 'It's hard to earn
ah shtickale broit, a piece of bread.
But listen, who needs to speak from this so early?'

"Instead your father and his friends talked from other subjects.

They speaked about Korea, the Suez Canal, Israel, the American elections, China, Hungary..."

"America never will build ah SPUTNIK. This I can guarantee you."

"I hear the Russians want also to send a DOG into the heavens."

"Maybe this animal will find GOD for them? Who knows? Ha, ha."

Sure enough, on November 3, 1957, one month after Sputnik One, the Russians launched Sputnik Two, with LAIKA the dog on board.

Yes, Daddy's friends stopped in for their newspapers, cigarettes...and to chat. They conducted earnest discussions about the weather, politics, jokes, gossip...

"I tell you, **Mattaleh,** if you put them in the **U.N.,** I'm sure they would fix all the problems from the world! Who needs to buy a newspaper? With them talking, who needs even to hear a **radio?**"

(The store radio, in fact, was always on and tuned to **WEVD**—
"the station that speaks your language.")

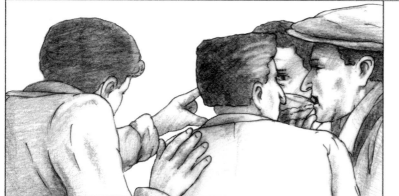

HIS friends were happy in **America.**

Not so Daddy.

He hungered for the good old days—specifically, his time in the army of the great SOVIET UNION.

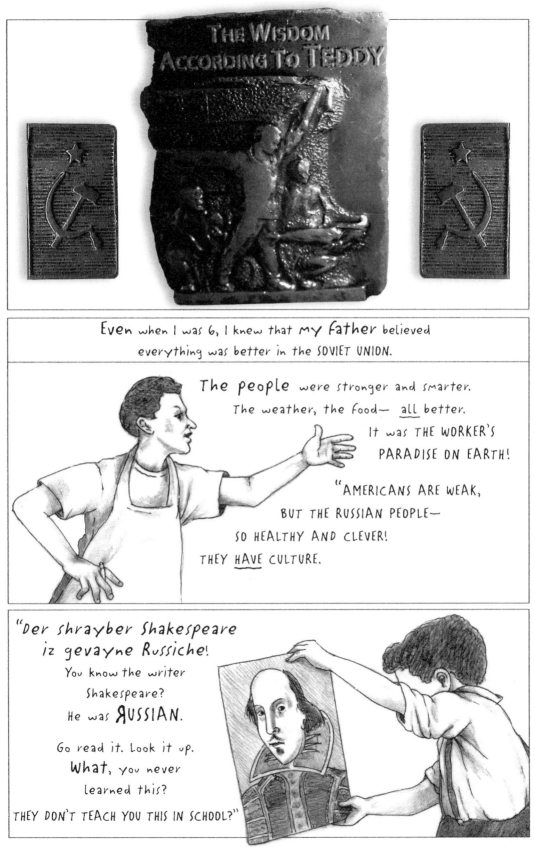

THE WISDOM ACCORDING TO TEDDY

Even when I was 6, I knew that MY FATHER believed everything was better in the SOVIET UNION.

The people were stronger and smarter. The weather, the food— all better.
It was THE WORKER'S PARADISE ON EARTH!

"AMERICANS ARE WEAK, BUT THE RUSSIAN PEOPLE— SO HEALTHY AND CLEVER! THEY HAVE CULTURE.

"Der shrayber Shakespeare iz gevayne Russiche!
You know the writer Shakespeare? He was RUSSIAN.

Go read it. Look it up. What, you never learned this?
THEY DON'T TEACH YOU THIS IN SCHOOL?"

Heaven forbid if you said a bad word about STALIN in front of Daddy.

"That man is some leader!" he says.

EARLY ONE MORNING...

"How is it you can like a man like Stalin?" asks the Deli man. "Did you forget he signed an agreement with Hitler— WITH HITLER! How can a good man do such a thing?"

MY FATHER GLARES, SHAKES HIS FIST, WAGGLES HIS FINGER, AND YELLS, "IDIOT! IMBECILE! DIDN'T YOU KNOW STALIN WAS TRICKING HITLER? All along Stalin knows what he is doing! He knows what's good for the Russian peoples. He is like a Father."

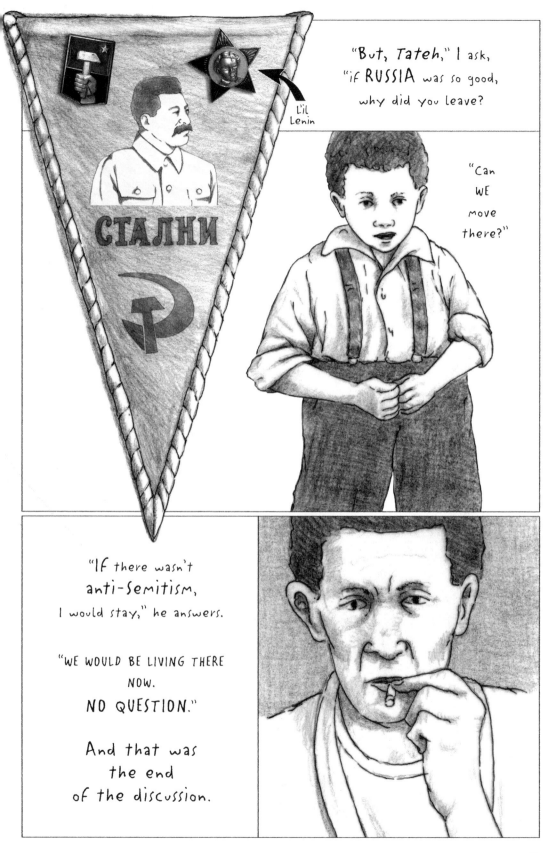

"But, *Tateh*," I ask, "if RUSSIA was so good, why did you leave?

L'il Lenin

СТАЛНИ

"Can WE move there?"

"If there wasn't anti-Semitism, I would stay," he answers.

"WE WOULD BE LIVING THERE NOW. NO QUESTION."

And that was the end of the discussion.

"Mattaleh, your father is a crazy person! Tell me, what country is so good, like AMERICA?"

Mommy, Bernard, and I walk a few blocks north on Howard Avenue.

There's a crowd. Someone sticks an AMERICAN flag in my hand, and as Eisenhower drives by in a big car, I wave it... IT'S THE 1956 ELECTION CAMPAIGN!

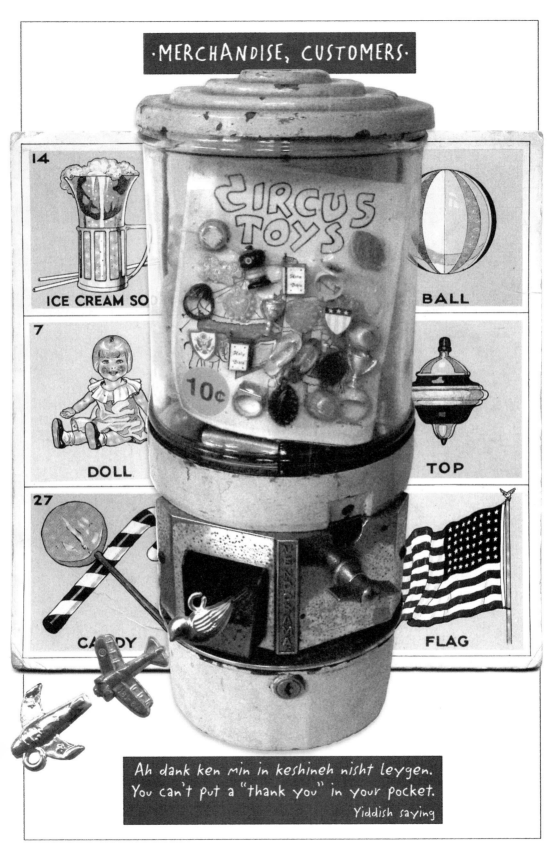

·MERCHANDISE, CUSTOMERS·

14 ICE CREAM SODA

7 DOLL

27 CANDY

CIRCUS TOYS

10¢

BALL

TOP

FLAG

Ah dank ken min in keshineh nisht leygen.
You can't put a "thank you" in your pocket.
Yiddish saying

93

·7:30 am·

Sleepy children crowd into **TEDDY'S** for early morning **DRINKS, TOYS,** and **CANDY.**

It's only half a block from **PS 12**— the neighborhood school.

NO 12 PUBLIC SCHOOL

BY 8:30 the store is mobbed. Then, by 9:00, it's quiet.

The rush begins again around 3pm— when school lets out.

After that, business is pretty steady until dark.

"VAT YOU VANT YOU LITTLE BESTETS!" growls Teddy.

"IT'S FUNNY," a little girl observes.

"He speaks a foreign language."

DADDY'S CURSING
didn't
rattle the **kids**.
They understood that
as long as their **money** was out,
<u>and</u> they were ready to buy,
everything was A-OK
with
MISTER TEDDY.

"**His bark** is worse than **his bite**," kids say.

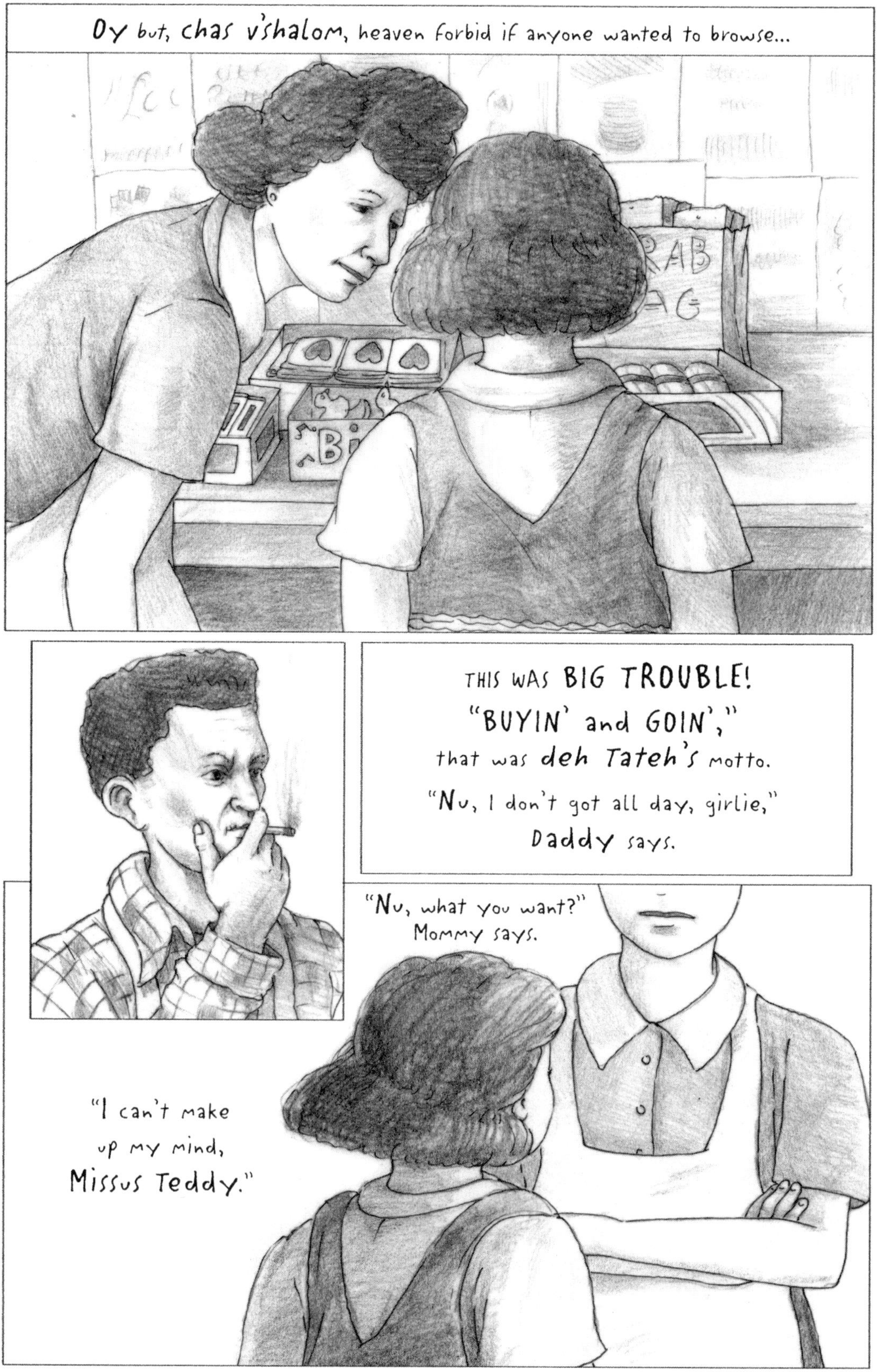
Oy but, chas v'shalom, heaven forbid if anyone wanted to browse...
THIS WAS BIG TROUBLE!
"BUYIN' and GOIN',"
that was deh Tateh's motto.
"Nu, I don't got all day, girlie,"
Daddy says.
"Nu, what you want?"
Mommy says.
"I can't make
up my mind,
Missus Teddy."

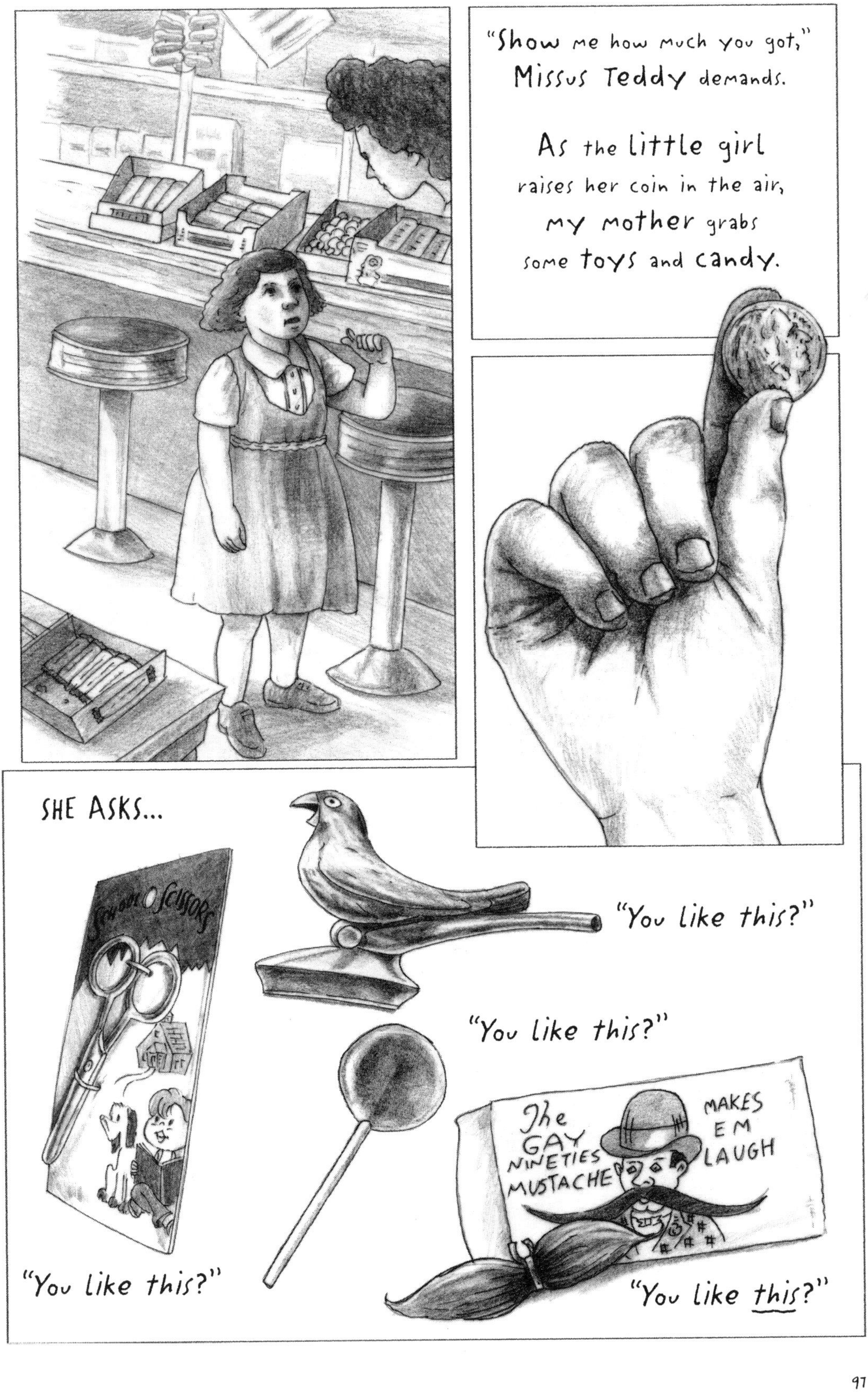

"Show me how much you got," Missus Teddy demands.
As the little girl raises her coin in the air, my mother grabs some toys and candy.
SHE ASKS...
SCHOOL SCISSORS
"You like this?"
"You like this?"
"You like this?"
The GAY NINETIES MUSTACHE
MAKES EM LAUGH
"You like this?"

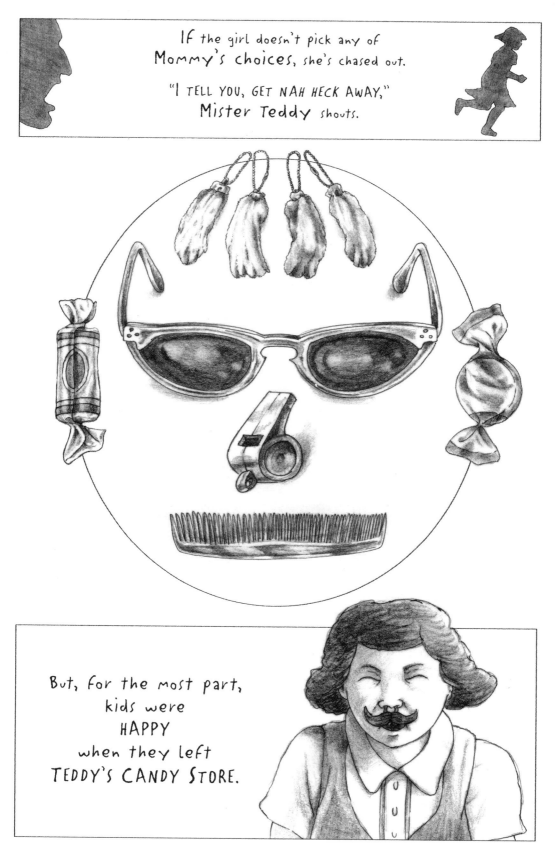

If the girl doesn't pick any of
Mommy's choices, she's chased out.

"I TELL YOU, GET NAH HECK AWAY,"
Mister Teddy shouts.

But, for the most part,
kids were
HAPPY
when they left
TEDDY'S CANDY STORE.

-WHY NOT?-
A nickel got you
a lime rickey or a bottle of pop.

A PENNY OR TWO
KEPT YOU IN *DOTS* FOR DAYS.

When Teddy's first opened,
a customer could sit
at the counter and comfortably
enjoy a malted or a sundae.

As the years progressed, the counter
became covered with merchandise.

In addition to the expected boxes
of Chuckles, chocolate bars, candy necklaces,
candy cigarettes, Jujyfruits, wax lips,
balls, Pez, and bubble gum cigars, you'd find
bandages, antacid tablets, gloves...
odd sorts of items to stock
in a candy store.

After a while, just
2 or 3 inches was left
to park your ice cream soda.

We didn't just stock for kids.

"The young peoples was coming into the store, too," Daddy says. "We sold a lot **engagement rings**."

They were only 10 and 25 cents apiece.

"The **rings** was just like in a **jewelry store**," he says, "but **cheap**."

"Maybe, this ONE is for you?" Mister Teddy asks the teen couple. "So beautiful, <u>and</u> you can make bigger and smaller to fit the finger."

The **novelty rings** were packed in soft yellow foam— very fancy.

With the aid of a 25 cent ring, **my father**, was an unlikely CUPID.

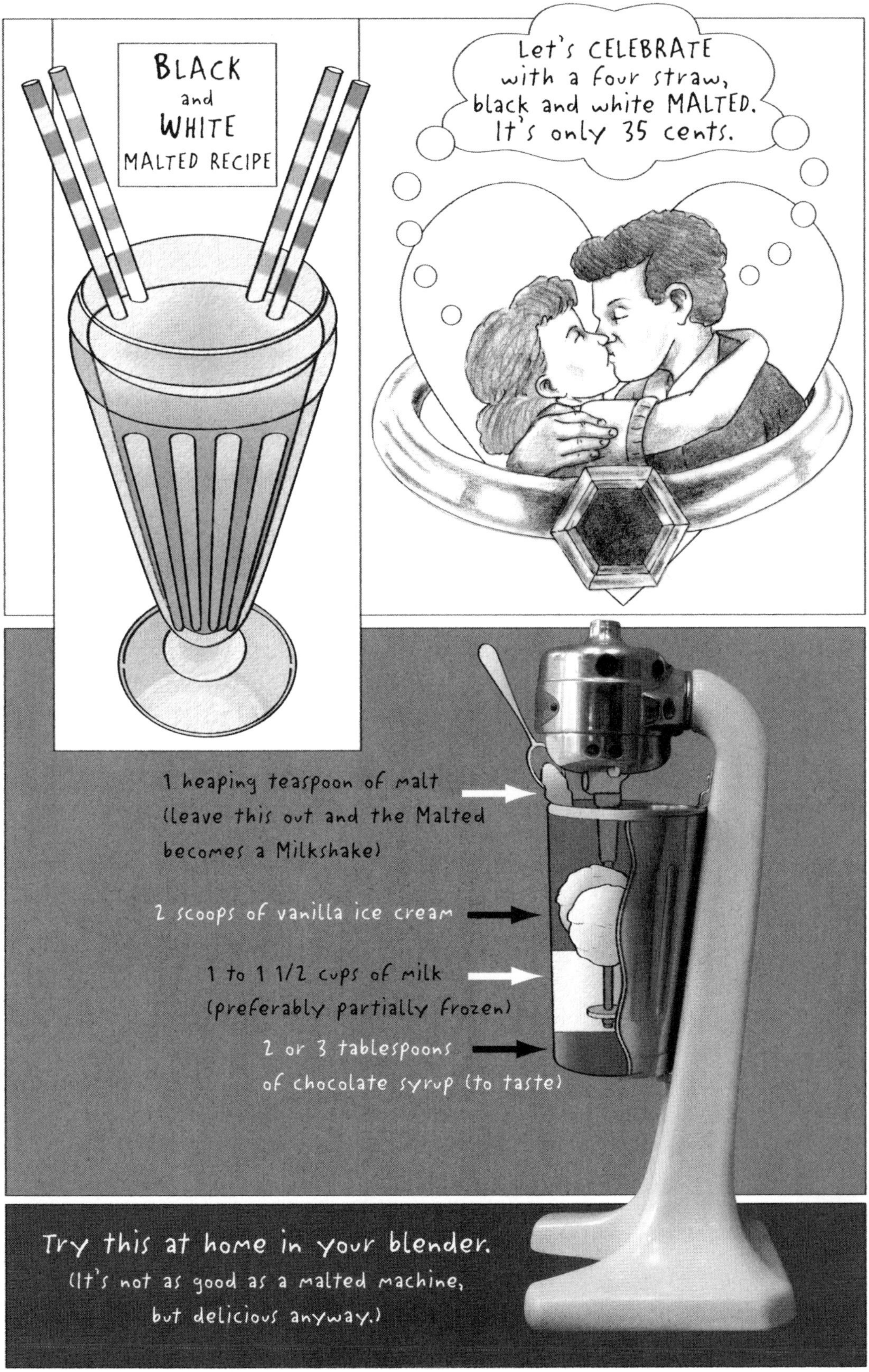
BLACK and WHITE MALTED RECIPE
Let's CELEBRATE with a four straw, black and white MALTED. It's only 35 cents.
1 heaping teaspoon of malt (leave this out and the Malted becomes a Milkshake)
2 scoops of vanilla ice cream
1 to 1 1/2 cups of milk (preferably partially frozen)
2 or 3 tablespoons of chocolate syrup (to taste)
Try this at home in your blender.
(It's not as good as a malted machine, but delicious anyway.)

"I sold many things in the store," says Daddy, "but ice cream, for sure, was my bread and butter."

CHOC CHIP

CHI LLA

STR RRY

PIS HIO

BUTT CAN

VAN DGE

"The ice cream we scooped was Dairy Crest— FIRST CLASS, THE BEST.
Next block was another candy store. They sold the Breyers...FEH.
Who can eat this? The vanilla has little black spots. Our vanilla was pure white."

"I have all flavors—
vanilla, chocolate, strawberry,
chocolate chip, mint,
vanilla fudge (this your mother likes),
even pistachio, butter pecan,
and more.
Sometimes we carried coconut,
banana, and peach.
I made fresh cones, pints, quarts.
We sold novelties—
ice cream pops, sandwiches, push-ups.

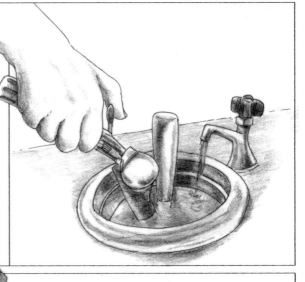

"In the summer
the peoples buy
rainbow ices, cherry ices,
lemon ices, coffee ices,
and bubble gum ices.
CHOCOLATE ICES
WE GOT ALL YEAR.
This was a big mover
for us."

"Your father was
a good-for-nothing,"
MOMMY says,
"but when he
worked
with ice cream,
he made excellent.

NO ONE COULD
MAKE BETTER."

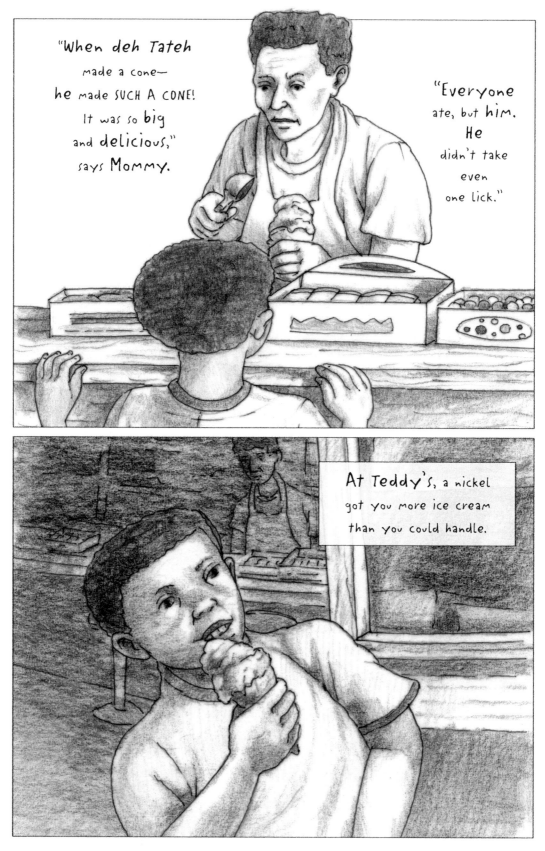

"When deh Tateh made a cone— he made SUCH A CONE! It was so big and delicious," says Mommy.

"Everyone ate, but him. He didn't take even one lick."

At Teddy's, a nickel got you more ice cream than you could handle.

"From all over they came to taste your **father's** ice cream sodas and FRAPPES," says Mommy.
"What's a **frappe**, you ask? Well, what you call now a **sundae**, we called ah **frop**, a **frappe**."

This was **THE PERFECT FOOD** —
a mountain of rich ice cream, chocolate syrup, honeyed walnuts, strawberry sauce, pineapples in syrup, and maybe, if **Daddy** felt like it, a couple of banana slices.

"You vant maybe vipped cream and ah cherry?"
Daddy asked **his customers.**
"You bet, Teddy!"
In the 1950s everyone wanted the maraschino cherry and whipped cream.

"Sure, **Mattaleh**—
deh whole world liked
mine **whip cream.**
I make good. No?"

(This cardboard sign doesn't even begin
to do the **frappe** justice.)

"My whip cream recipe is like this— 1 container heavy cream, a little vanilla ice cream and vanilla syrup... Nothing more. I put all These things in the **whip-cream machine**. Then I put in a BULLET and shake the machine. This is the same whip-cream maker I use for mine whole life."

The bullet is a → nitrous oxide cartridge.

← (I was so happy when I found Daddy's whipped cream machine in my garage. I thought I'd thrown it away years before. The rubber nozzle has rotted off with age.)

When no one was looking, I'd snatch the **whipped cream maker** from the refrigerator, shake it up and press the lever. WHIPPED CREAM OOZED INTO MY MOUTH. *Ah Mechayeh!* The best whipped cream I've ever tasted.

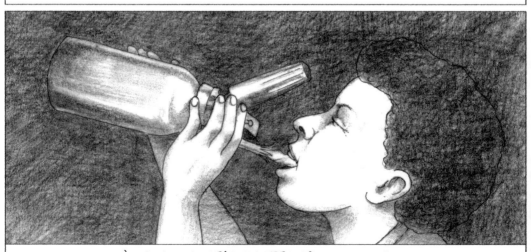

We're lucky the HEALTH INSPECTOR never caught me.

BUSINESS WAS PRETTY MUCH ROUND-THE-CLOCK.
All sorts of people came by...

THE SHNORER · דער שנארער

"Mattaleh," says Mommy, "do you remember all the **shnorers** in the neighborhood, all those **freeloaders**?

Oy, what these sly bandits did. Listen...

"**First**, one comes into the store and asks **the father** for a drink—maybe an **egg cream** or a **fountain Coca-Cola**.

"So, for sure, **the father** makes the man, let's say, an egg cream, just like he makes for everybody— DELICIOUS, just **proifect!**"

"The schnorer drinks.

"After he swallows
ah hulbeh glaysel,
a half a glass maybe,
he says,
'Teddy, maybe you will
fill me up with more seltzer?

You make too sweet
the drink.'"

If my father was in a good mood,
he added more seltzer.
More likely though, it's—
"Go out from my store, YOU LOUSY GONIFF!"

"Try a Delicious **Egg Cream** at Home!"

only **10¢**

Now with no Eggs _or_ Cream!

Fill with Seltzer

About this much milk

About this much Chocolate Syrup
—a little more couldn't hurt—

For more foam, direct Seltzer straight down and stir.

For less foam, direct Seltzer to side of cup while stirring.

Chocolate is the classic egg cream syrup.
I can also recommend VANILLA SYRUP. It's good, too!
But, don't try lime, strawberry, cherry, or Coke syrup.
I've experimented with them and they made me
want to throw up.

Oops, almost forgot...to prevent overflow,
stop pouring about 1.5 inches from the top of the glass.

"Der Tateh's landsleit, these greenhorns was sometimes very funny," says Mommy.

"They don't speak so good ENGLISH, like me."

Ma, why do you keep interrupting me? You're ruining MY STORY.

"Mattaleh, Mattaleh, you will have plenty of time to tell what YOU want to tell.

Listen, the peoples will like MY STORY. I promise, it will be short and they will laugh.

"This comedy is from an 'ambulance.'

HA! This is a good joke..."

"One day a man runs into the store. 'Goldie, Teddy,' he says, 'please, can you get for me an ambulance?'

'For sure, mister,' I say. 'I will call for you an ambulance. WHAT HAPPENED? Should we maybe call the police, too?

'Missis,' this shlimiel says, 'How can you CALL an ambulance? And for what do we NEED the police?'

He looks on me like I'm crazy!"

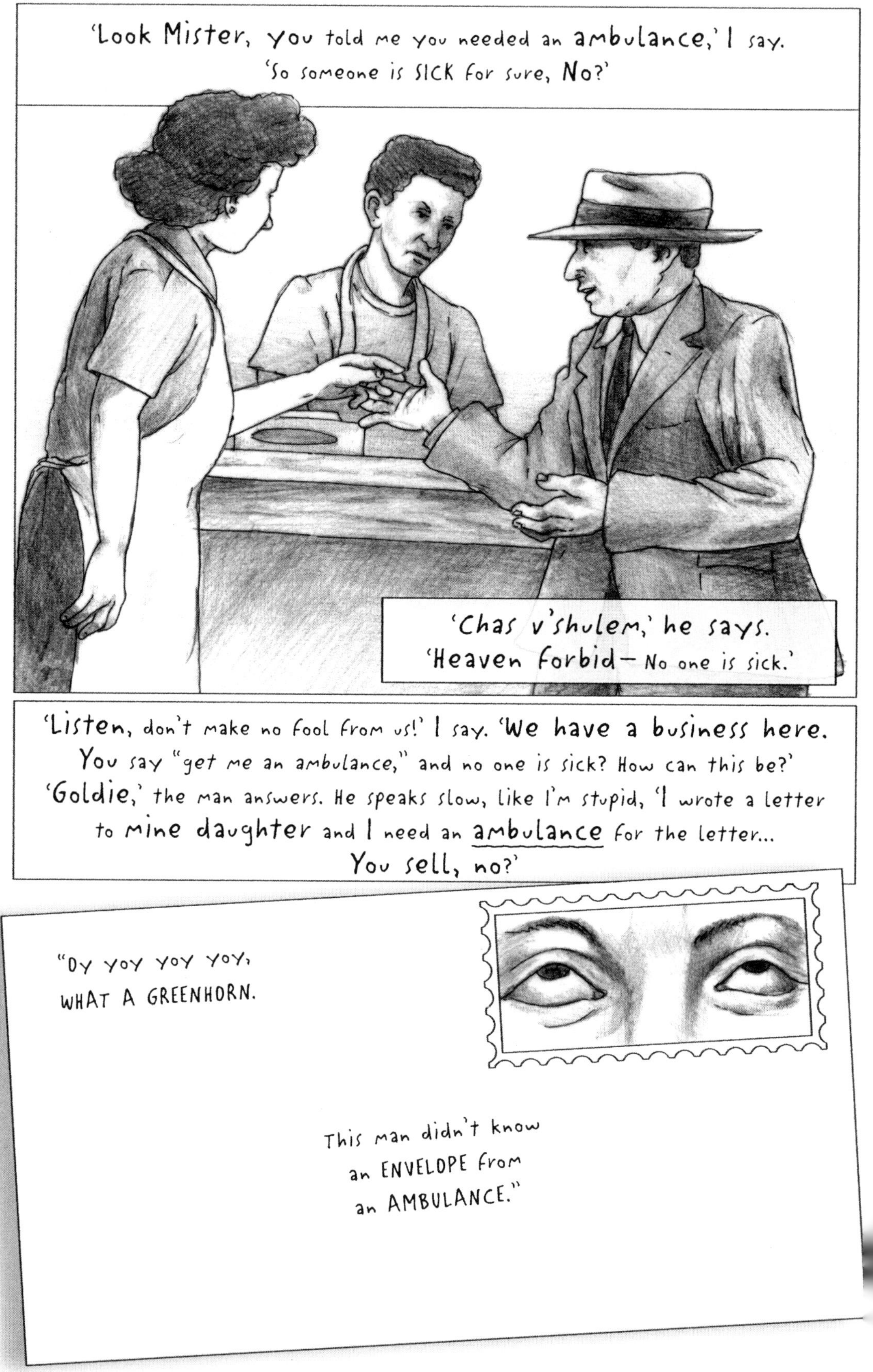
'Look Mister, you told me you needed an ambulance,' I say.
'So someone is SICK for sure, No?'
'Chas v'shulem,' he says.
'Heaven forbid— No one is sick.'
'Listen, don't make no fool from us!' I say. 'We have a business here.
You say "get me an ambulance," and no one is sick? How can this be?'
'Goldie,' the man answers. He speaks slow, like I'm stupid, 'I wrote a letter
to mine daughter and I need an ambulance for the letter...
You sell, no?'
"OY YOY YOY YOY,
WHAT A GREENHORN.
This man didn't know
an ENVELOPE from
an AMBULANCE."

Jews weren't our only customers in the 1950s.
Some Blacks, Puerto Ricans, Irish, and Italians live in the neighborhood, too.

"Mattaleh, I tell you who is a good customer. Do you remember Mister... Oh, I forget his name— is an Italian name. This man is so respectful. He comes every week for a **two cents plain** and a box **De Noblis.**"

"Such a nice day. Ain't it Missus Teddy?"

Although **El Producto** was our best-selling cigar, we had at least one customer for our crooked, foul-smelling **De Noblis.**

My Father Smoked like a chimney, but, the MISTER-WITH-THE-ITALIAN-NAME was my introduction to real **air pollution.**

"Such flavor!"

"Not everyone was so nice like this Italian man...

I'm reminding myself of a Puerto Rican lady— SHE SHOULD ONLY BURN IN HELL!

"When you was little, **Mattaleh**, you was very, very cute.
All the ladies say, 'GOLDIE, WHAT A BEAUTIFUL BOY YOU HAVE.'
I'm thinking, Oy vey iz mir, oh woe to me, my son will get a **Getoyk**,
you know— the **Evil Eye**.

In this time was the Puerto Rican lady— I thought a nice woman.
She has her own children but, still she couldn't get enough from you.
HER EYES WOULD EAT YOU UP.

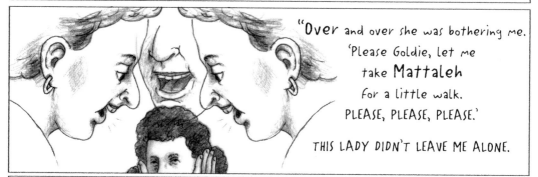

"Over and over she was bothering me.
'Please Goldie, let me take **Mattaleh** for a little walk.
PLEASE, PLEASE, PLEASE.'

THIS LADY DIDN'T LEAVE ME ALONE.

"So one time,
when the store was very busy,
I told her, YES.

I said, 'Sure, Missus, take him out for a walk,
but YOU BRING HIM BACK SOON.
OK?'"

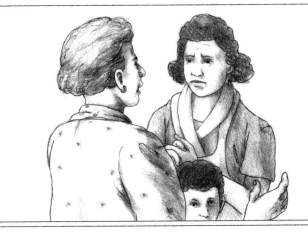

'OF COURSE, GOLDIE,
WE WILL BE BACK SOON.
DON'T YOU WORRY,
I WILL WATCH OVER
MATTALEH,'
she says,
'LIKE A HAWK.'

"1 hour passes. 2 hours pass. 3 hours pass. 4 HOURS PASS...
I'M GOING CRAZY.

"I'm thinking,
'What did I do?
I'm such a stupid woman.
DID THIS WOMAN KIDNAP
MY BABY?
Tovia is going to kill me.
Why was I born?
I don't deserve to live!'

All these things was JUMPING
in my head.

"Finally...
This lady came back—
full with apologies.
'Please forgive me, Goldie.
I forgot the time!'
she says.
'I'M SO SORRY,' SHE SAYS.
'And Mattaleh
played so nice
with my children.'"

"**OY**, did I give it to her! 'How you could do this to me?' I said.

'DID YOU WANT TO KILL ME? Isn't it enough for you that I lost my whole family in the War?'"

So where was I? What did I do for 4 hours?

Did I climb the steps in the PUERTO RICAN LADY'S apartment building?

Did I visit her apartment?

Did I play with her children?

HONESTLY, I DON'T REMEMBER.

I DON'T KNOW.

What I do know is that from then, until now, I can count from 1 to 10 in Spanish.

"Uno, dos, tres, quatro, cinco, seis, siete, ocho, nueve, diez."

"Sometimes Mattaleh, you caused so many problems," says Mommy. "Because of you, we almost lost a good customer."

I CAN STILL SEE HIM, GLARING AT ME. HE HATES ME.

"This man was wearing a suit and a tie everyday— a fine colored gentleman— married to a sweet white lady. He buys only expensive toys for his childrens.

'You Jews have America all figured out, Teddy,' he says. 'After only 10 years here, you all make a good life for your families.

We Negroes are here 400 years, and we have yet to figure it out. THE WHITES DON'T LET US. WE DON'T LET OURSELVES.'

'America, feh,' Daddy says. 'The black people would be better off in Russia. There everyone is...'

'Excuse me, mister,' I interrupt. 'How come you're black and your wife is white?'

(A biracial couple wasn't something I saw everyday.)

If not for this man liking your father, I think he would have KILLED YOU."

And then there was Stacy...

"Hey, Teddy, I got enough for 2 singles."

He came in to get his "smokes" and shoot the breeze with Daddy.

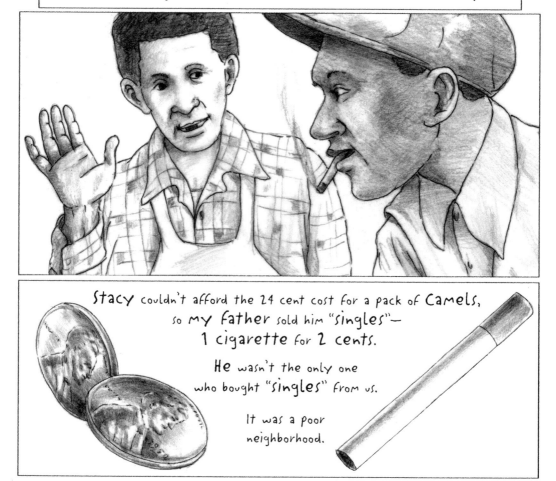

Stacy couldn't afford the 24 cent cost for a pack of Camels, so my father sold him "singles"— 1 cigarette for 2 cents.

He wasn't the only one who bought "singles" from us.

It was a poor neighborhood.

"You wouldn't believe," says Mommy, "but Stacy spoke Yiddish with the father."

אַ גוט מרגען טעדי. וואָס מאַכט איר.

Gut morning, Stacy. Vat's cookin'?

"Stacy learned to talk from **deh Tateh** and all the other Jewish storekeepers in the neighborhood. IN RETURN, HE TEACHED YOUR FATHER ENGLISH."

YOU TAUGHT ME LANGUAGE, AND MY PROFIT ON'T IS, I KNOW HOW TO CURSE.*

*CALIBAN— THE TEMPEST

STACY was a very good English teacher. Soon, *bestet* and *sahnahvabitch* were critical parts of my father's everyday vocabulary.

"NO Teddy, try it again— BASTARD, not BESTET."

"Why are you hocking mer a chinik*?

I said BESTET, exactly like YOU told me!"

*literally— "Hitting me a teakettle."

"You know, Mattaleh, don't forget, I was coming to the store, too," my Uncle Isia says. "Maybe 2-3 times a week.

"I and **Jenny** and **my children** lived just a couple blocks away.

"**After** a time I stopped coming. There was a coldness I was feeling from **your father**— not so much bad words, just COLDNESS.

"I was thinking that **we** went through so much, **your mother** and **me**, and **she** and **your father** don't invite me even ONCE into the back of the store to maybe have a CUP of COFFEE in **your kitchen**."

"How could we invite Isia or ANYONE to visit us in the back?" my mother asks.

"Between the boxes, we lived in filth.

It's funny— Isia wanted to sit in the kitchen to drink a cup coffee.

"WHO HAD A KITCHEN TABLE?"

I knew I couldn't invite friends to play at "OUR HOUSE."

First Simon,

then Isia,

then Yetala.

I only knew them because of the **photographs** in **my mother's nighttable**—
And I heard about them when my parents fought.

When I think about what **my mother** and **father** experienced during the WAR,
it's impossible for me to understand how they could have cut themselves off
from their only surviving relatives. TO ME THIS WAS CRAZY.

"Mattaleh, we was ALL CRAZY,"
my Uncle Isia says.
"To go through the fire
we went through and to be
a normal person—
there is not a generation
that can do it.
How many days we went hungry,
and every minute you don't know
if a bullet will come.
Who knew if we will make it
through the night?

NO ONE KNEW."

·PURE PROFIT·

Az meh hut gelt, iz men klug, un shain, un meh ken gut zingen.
If you have money, you're wise, good looking and can sing well.

Yiddish saying

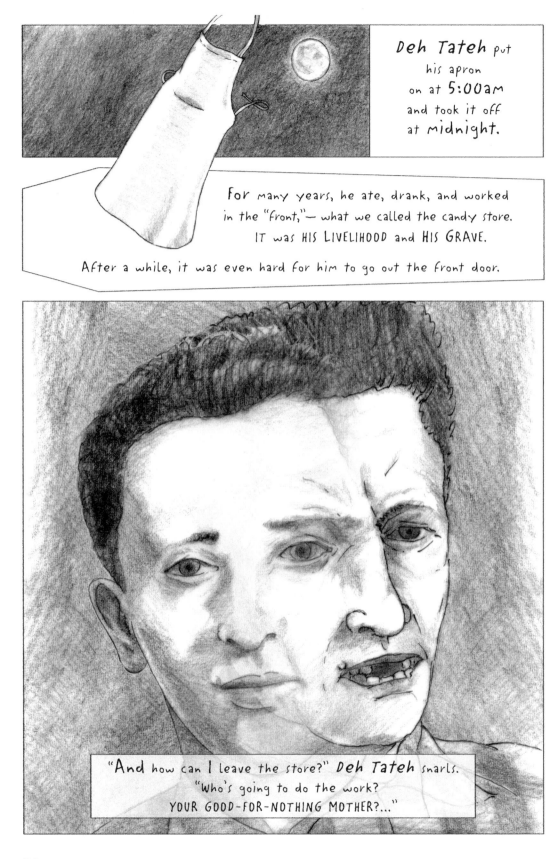

Deh Tateh put his apron on at 5:00am and took it off at midnight.

For many years, he ate, drank, and worked in the "front,"— what we called the candy store.
IT was HIS LIVELIHOOD and HIS GRAVE.

After a while, it was even hard for him to go out the front door.

"And how can I leave the store?" Deh Tateh snarls.
"Who's going to do the work?
YOUR GOOD-FOR-NOTHING MOTHER?..."

He left only
when he had to
"MAKE BUSINESS"
with the CANDY
and TOY
WHOLESALERS—
to buy *schoira*,
merchandise.

Bernard
and I
joined him
on those trips.

We'd set off for downtown Brooklyn or the lower East Side of Manhattan.

"Always,
I was working
in the store with
the father,"
my mother
says.

"When **he**
was not there,
I take care of
the store
REAL GOOD!"

For Daddy,
our DAY OUT
was just another part
of his struggle
to make a living.

For me, though,
it was
an adventure!...

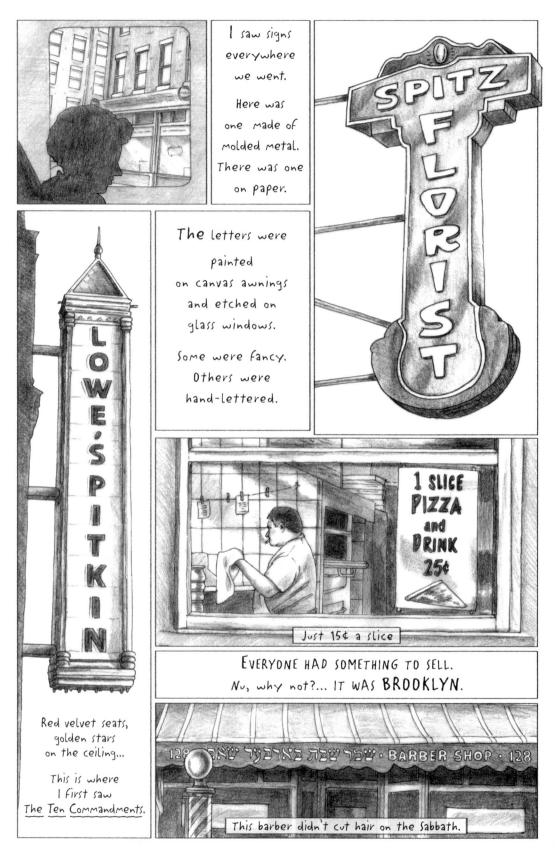

I saw signs everywhere we went.

Here was one made of molded metal. There was one on paper.

SPITZ FLORIST

The letters were painted on canvas awnings and etched on glass windows.

Some were fancy. Others were hand-lettered.

LOWE'S PITKIN

Red velvet seats, golden stars on the ceiling...

This is where I first saw The Ten Commandments.

1 SLICE PIZZA and DRINK 25¢

Just 15¢ a slice

EVERYONE HAD SOMETHING TO SELL. Nu, why not?... IT WAS BROOKLYN.

שמר שבת בארבע שאר · BARBER SHOP · 128

This barber didn't cut hair on the Sabbath.

THIS was always our FIRST STOP.

Daddy goes into the store.

"Blayb du," he says. "Stay here."

And so we wait outside.

Inside he buys 2 small bottles of VODKA.

"Hmm, they look just like the tiny wax bottles filled with colored syrup that we sell," I tell Bernard.

Daddy was finished even before he left the store.

He didn't DRINK— he SUCKED, he INHALED.

Now, he was ready to hondel, you know— to deal.

It was time to meet with the wholesalers.

"How much for a gross novelties, 2 dozen lunchboxes, 3 dozen assorted..."

After a few hours of bargaining, **deh Tateh**'s inspired.

He starts buying items you'd see in hardware stores, pharmacies, luncheonettes...

"Gimme a gross combs, a dozen ladies winter gloves, a carton antacid tablets. Maybe you got hammers, extension cords?"

OUR LONG DAY ENDS, AND WE HEAD HOME, TO THE STORE.

"This candy store was a hard job for me and the father. It was like we was working 24 hours a day.

A day off, you don't see. We close only for Rosh Hashanah, Yom Kippur, and one day from Pesach.

"Normal peoples was going to shul on Shabbos.

"But no, der Tateh wants the store open all the time— AH REAL MESHUGGENER...

He was only thinking from makin' money."

"Mattaleh, come here. I want you to look on this."

Daddy shows me a carton of CHICLETS—included inside are an extra 4 dozen penny packages of the gum.

"Did you know the Candy companies give bonuses if you buy a lot of moichindise? FREE from CHARGE," he says proudly.

"This is my reward for being a good customer You see, Mattaleh, PURE PROFIT!"

48 cents of PURE PROFIT...

"Why you always make fun from us, Mattaleh?"
my mother says. "THIS IS NOT FAIR.
We sell a lot of goods and we make a living."

Jan. 12, 1960

TO WHOM IT MAY CONCERN :

Mr. Touia Lemelman has earned the net income for the corresponding

years listed below.

YEAR	NET INCOME
1957	$ 3180.00
1958	3050.00
1959	3250.00

Very truly yours,

I found this document about a month after
my mother died.
I think it was a letter from their lawyer to the IRS.

·INFESTED·

TIP TOP
SPIDER
MADE IN HONG KONG

Plastic
MADE IN HONG KONG

HUNTERS WALKING BEETLE
really running
Life-Alike
MADE IN HONG KONG

Beim oiskeren di shtub, gefint min allis.
When you sweep the house, you find everything.

Yiddish saying

132

·MY FIRST MEMORY·

I'M HOLDING A
DEAD MOUSE.

Its coat is fuzzy.

The tail twirls
between
my thumb
and
index finger.

I can't see it when I close my eyes. I CAN FEEL IT.

I've tried, but can't seem to remember how I killed it.

Bernard tells me I used a shoe.

He was 7. I was 4.

What I can't forget is the sound of Mommy and Daddy screaming at me.

"VUS BIST DU MESHUGAH? WHAT ARE YOU CRAZY?" they shriek.

"How can you bring a dead mouse into the store?

This is a business! We have customers!"

Oy vey. I thought they would be pleased. Why weren't they proud of me? It's not so easy to hit a MOUSE.

THEY SHOULD TRY IT SOMETIME!

"Mattaleh, you got a mouse story. I got a rat story," Daddy says.

"HEHR ZACH TZU. NOW, YOU LISTEN."

"One day, maybe 11 o'clock in the morning, we was slow in the store. Your mother was taking care and I go in the back, pardon me, tzu pishin...

"After I finished, I found a BIG DEAD RAT on the floor near the steam. I know I have to throw THIS outside in the street, in the garbage. BUT, I was thinking that our customers don't need to know we was having RATS. For sure, we would lose business.

"So I wrapped it GOOD in newspaper, and put it in a bag— the customers shouldn't see when I take the RAT out to the garbage."

"SO WHAT HAPPENED NEXT?

When I come to the front, I am seeing we was busy. Just like this.

One minute we don't have no customers, the next minute we was crowded.

"NOW, I can't take my bag outside to throw out.

Instead, I put it down on a chair and I dealt with the shoppers."

"Maybe a half hour later, the store was empty from peoples.

NOW I COULD THROW OUT THE RAT.

But... when I looked on the chair, the bag was no more there.

SOMEBODY STEALED IT.

"Who would think such a *mishigas* is ever possible?

I HOPE THIS THIEF HAD A GOOD SURPRISE WHEN HE OPENED UP HIS PRESENT!"

·A PRESENT FOR ME·

Yesterday morning I found
a **butterfly** near
the **store**— an unusual sight.

It was dead, but still...
I was happy to find it.
The butterfly was
perfect, complete.

EVEN ITS LEGS AND ANTENNAE WERE STILL ATTACHED.

Must have taken a wrong turn somewhere...

After all, there aren't any flowers growing in front of **TEDDY'S**.

It was with a real sense of **delight** that I showed everyone **my find.**

(I made up my mind to **keep it forever.**)

"*Gib* a kik," I say. "Take a look."

"You want to keep always?" **Daddy** asks. "I know how. I teach you how.

"*Hehr* zach tzu, **Mattaleh**," he says. "Put it in a book. Close it up and let stay a week.

After, will be dry, flat— *proifect—* You can keep forever."

An expert on these subjects— he spoke with such confidence...

139

As soon as I shut the book, I heard the sickening crunch of my butterfly's body.

Slowly, the insect juices spread across the pages.

BOY, WAS I ANGRY!

"WHY DID YOU MAKE ME RUIN MY BUTTERFLY?" I yell.

"YOU DON'T KNOW WHAT YOU'RE TALKING ABOUT!"

Deh Tateh remained unfazed.

"Mattaleh, Mattaleh," he tut-tutted, "you just didn't do it right. You have to listen better. Now go play with Jan. I got work."

As usual, that was the end of the discussion.

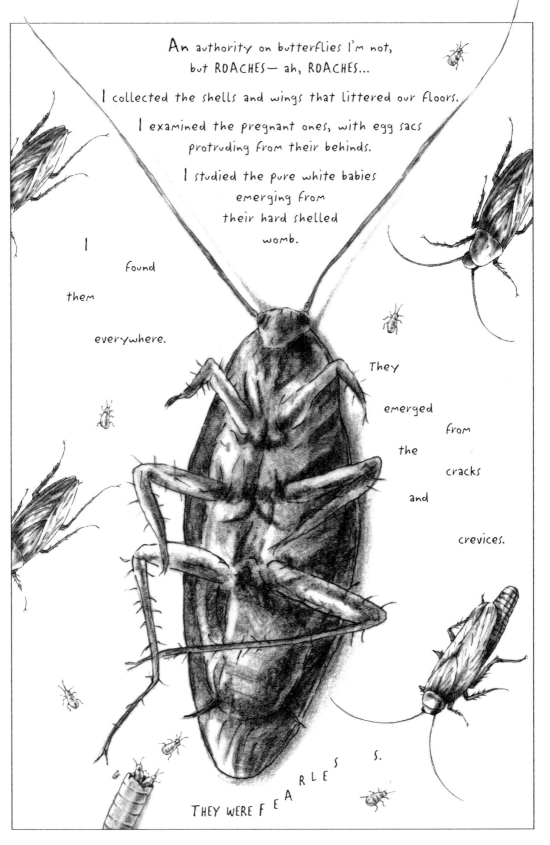

An authority on butterflies I'm not,
but ROACHES— ah, ROACHES...

I collected the shells and wings that littered our floors.

I examined the pregnant ones, with egg sacs
protruding from their behinds.

I studied the pure white babies
emerging from
their hard shelled
womb.

I
found

them

everywhere.

They

emerged

from

the

cracks

and

crevices.

THEY WERE F E A R L E S S.

141

In fact, our rooms were pretty much infested with, you name it, MICE, RATS, ANTS...

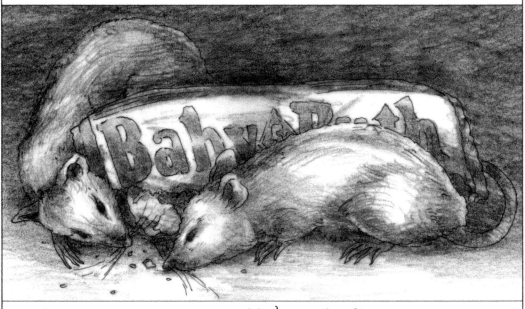

They made life unpleasant in Teddy's Candy Store. But, interesting.

Attracted
to the sweet candy,
the dried syrup,
and general disorder,
these pests
were cunning.
Like magicians' rabbits,
they appeared
and disappeared at will.

142

· SUMMER 1956 — Cock-a-Roach Dreams ·

BEFORE SUNRISE—
It was already hot.

The windows
have been
open all night.
But not even
the light breeze
that moves slowly
past the bars,
brings much relief.

I'm dreaming...

Dreaming that I'm dancing, running, jumping, splashing through the fire hydrant spray.

Squishy shoes—
I'm cool.
I'm wet.
I'm happy.

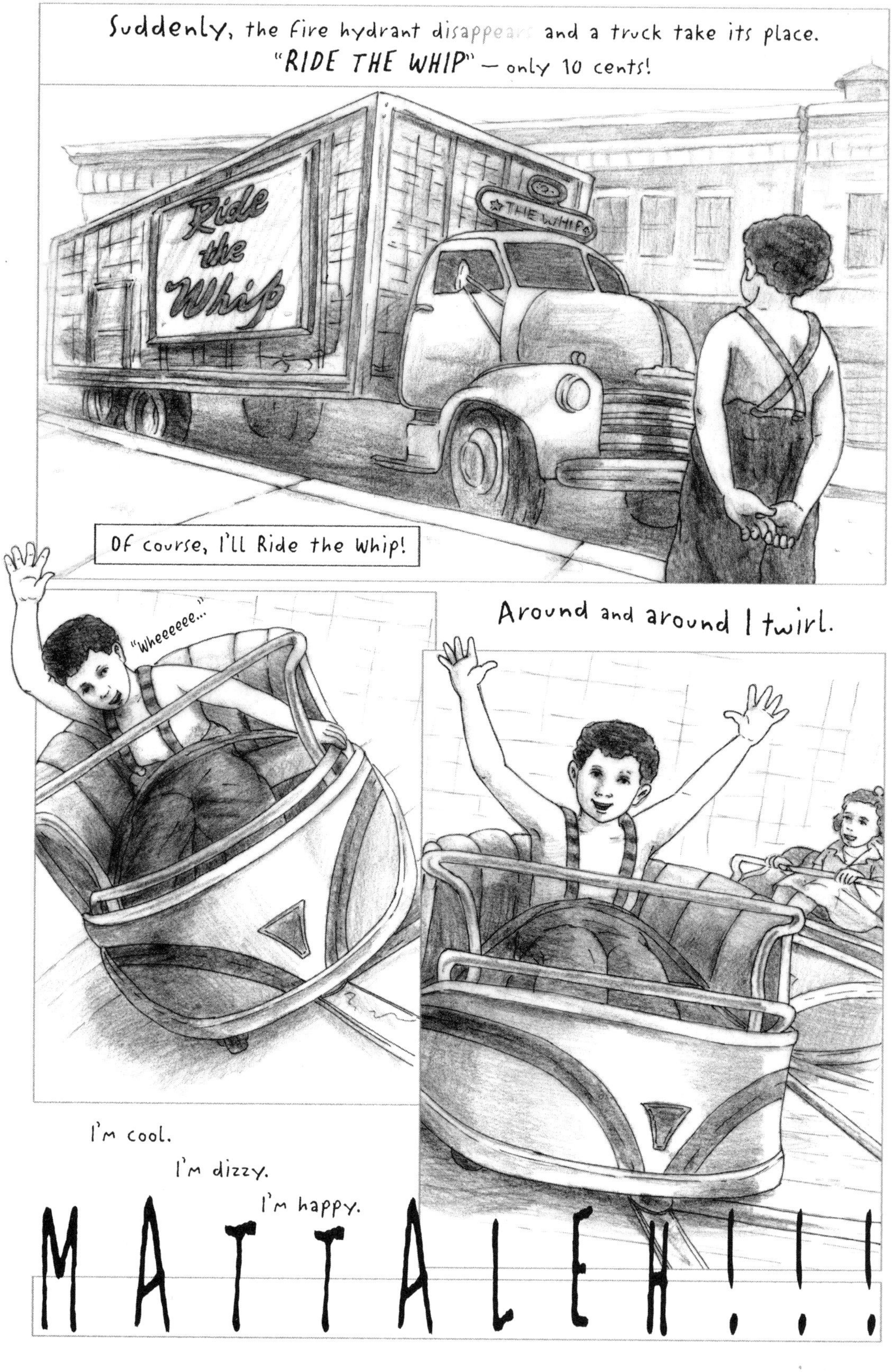
Suddenly, the fire hydrant disappears and a truck take its place.
"RIDE THE WHIP" — only 10 cents!
Ride the Whip
THE WHIP
Of course, I'll Ride the Whip!
"Wheeeeee..."
Around and around I twirl.
I'm cool.
I'm dizzy.
I'm happy.
MATTALEH!!!

JUST THEN, MOMMY'S FACE CUTS INTO MY SWEET DREAM.

"MATTALEH, YOU COME HERE RIGHT NOW!" she yells. "You need a 'whip' like a hole in the head. You will throw up from this! And the fire hydrant— Oy, are you crazy? WHY YOU NEED THE SPLASHING? Do you want, you should catch a cold? This is NOT for a nice Jewish boy. Let the *Goyim* run through the sprinkler."

"But Mommy, it's hot, and the water's nice."

"IF you're so hot MISTER, why don't you go into the store and *DER TATEH* will make you a nice ice cream soda."

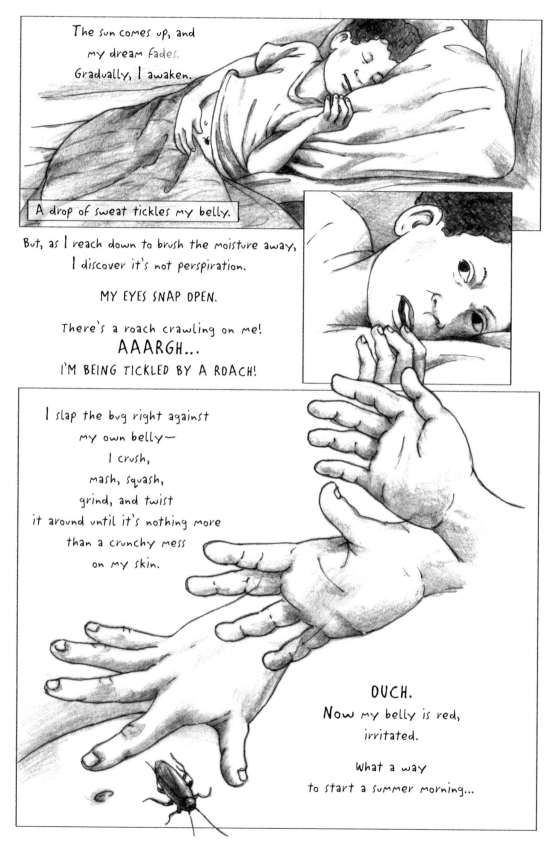

The sun comes up, and my dream fades. Gradually, I awaken.

A drop of sweat tickles my belly.

But, as I reach down to brush the moisture away, I discover it's not perspiration.

MY EYES SNAP OPEN.

There's a roach crawling on me!
AAARGH...
I'M BEING TICKLED BY A ROACH!

I slap the bug right against my own belly—
I crush,
mash, squash,
grind, and twist
it around until it's nothing more
than a crunchy mess
on my skin.

OUCH.
Now my belly is red, irritated.

What a way
to start a summer morning...

ROACHES were
with us all year.
ANTS?
They were seasonal.
They arrived in the Spring
and were gone by Fall.

In season, though,
we found them EVERYWHERE—
in the front of the store,
in the back.

I squashed hundreds and hundreds
until...

"Hmm," I think. "They'd make good pets."

So I squeezed a bunch through the broken
glass top of a toy novelty and
drop in a few grains
of sugar.
   VOILÁ!
   MY OWN
   ANT FARM.

Unfortunately, I forget
to give them water.

I hid my pets in the oven—
no one was going to look
for them there.

Sadly though, in a few days
they were all dead.

So, I shook the old ones out
and added new ones— but
with the same results.

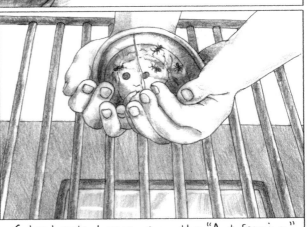

After about a month, and dozens of dead pets, I gave up on the "Ant Farming."

"Mrs. Lemelman, maybe you would like a pet for der kinder?"

·LI'L RIN TIN TIN·

One day, a nice lady gives us a German Shepherd puppy.

YAY!

Almost immediately it starts shitting EVERYWHERE!
We don't get a dog—
We get a crap factory!

"Oy, this is too much work for me," Mommy moans.

To contain him a little, we keep the puppy in our bathroom at night.

"One time I woke up to pee," Bernard remembers.
"I had to go really bad.
Then, when I opened the door to the toilet, I saw two puppies.
For a second I thought I was suffering from double vision,
but then it came to me...
One was our puppy and the other one was a big rat!

I quickly shut the bathroom door and held it in until morning."

A week later
my puppy vanishes...

"Mameh, where is deh hunt?" I ask.

"I gave him to 'your friend' Yankaleh,"
she tells me.
"Der hunt will have a better life
in his apartment.
In back of the store
is no life for a dog."

I'M SO ANGRY.
She didn't even ask
if I was willing
to give him up.

Afterwards,
MOMMY gives me
a genuine plastic Rin Tin Tin—
my consolation prize...
And that actually does
make me feel a little better.

The puppy dies 2 weeks later—
Hit by a car while
running away from Yankaleh.

"I HATE YOU, YANKALEH!
I HATE YOU!"

That plastic Rin Tin Tin now lives in my art studio— broken leg, chipped ears and all.

"THE MICE AND RATS ARE DRIVING ME CRAZY," Mommy wails.

"Who can live like this?"

So she buys a guaranteed mouse hunter.

Bernard and I name it CAT.

SHE WAS A SKILLED KILLER AND ALSO OUR PET.

After CAT we only shared 448 Howard Avenue with the ROACHES and ANTS.

I loved the way CAT
curled her body
around my legs and purred.

I loved the feel of her tongue
when she licked my hand.

She was a sweet cat—
sweet but also
very, _very_ sneaky.

CAT'S job was catching rats and mice.

BUT HER PASSION WAS SCARING THE HELL
OUT OF DOGS.

She always seemed
to know
when one was around.

Cat patiently waited under the soda bottle shelves...

Then, at the perfect moment, she leapt from her hiding place and jumped on her unsuspecting prey. She raked its back with sharp claws.

It was beautiful to behold— a Brooklyn ballet.

In the blink of an eye, CAT was back under the shelves, ready for her next victim.

"YOU GOT A CRAZY CAT THERE, TEDDY!"

Word spreads and customers start
tying up their pets before they come into the store.

CAT was very independent.
When night came,
she took off.
She wandered the streets,
looking for
cat companions.

ONE MORNING, IN 1962, CAT DIDN'T COME BACK.

MOMMY
found
her dying
in the street—
run over by a car.

I never saw
Mommy
cry so hard.

·THE REAL EVIL EYE·

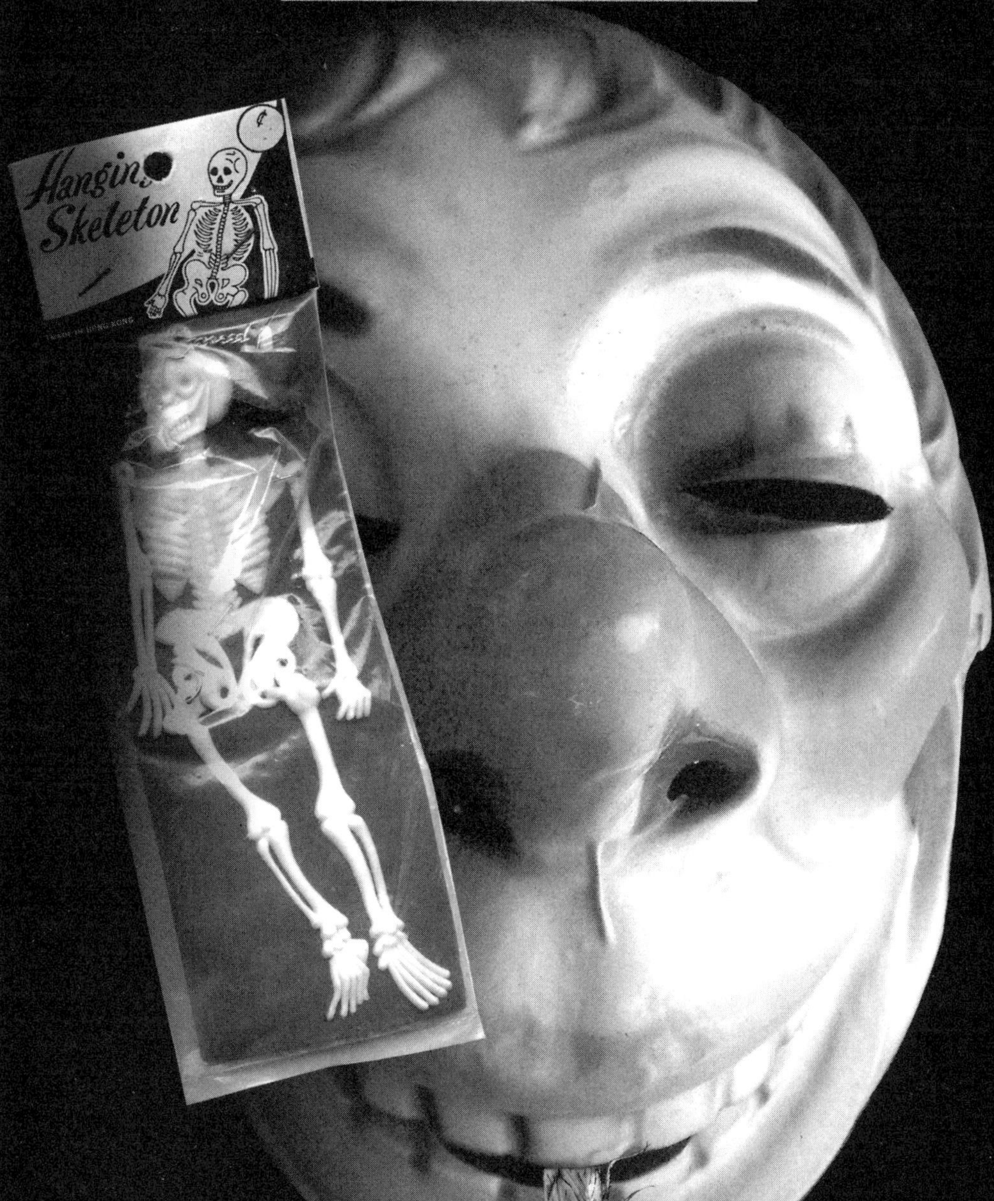
Skeleton

Der tsorin iz in hartzen ah doren.

Rage is a thorn in the heart.

Yiddish saying

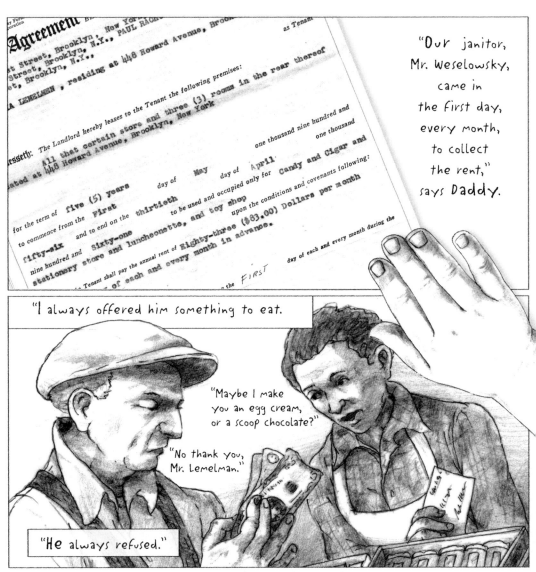

"Our janitor, Mr. Weselowsky, came in the first day, every month, to collect the rent," says Daddy.

"I always offered him something to eat.

"Maybe I make you an egg cream, or a scoop chocolate?"

"No thank you, Mr. Lemelman."

"He always refused."

"Mr. Weselowsky was a fine man," says Mommy. "He spoke with us in Polish. Once in a while he fixed for us something in the store."

Every week, like clockwork, MR. WESELOWSKY floated up out of the cellar, carrying a trash can full of coal ash from the boiler.

I ALWAYS WANTED TO GO DOWN THERE.

"Mattaleh, don't even think from going down to the cellar! You gonna fall down the steps and kill yourself."

·FORBIDDEN TERRITORY·

HA— MOMMY WAS WRONG!
I didn't kill myself.

But, if you look carefully, you'll see a thin white scar under my lip.
(If we ever meet, I'll show it to you.)

Here's what happened...

"Sure you could keep the empty syrup bottles in the cellar," Mr. Weselowsky tells Daddy. "No problem, Mr. Lemelman," he says. "We got plenty room."

Daddy stored them there until the "soda man" came with a new delivery. Daddy got credit for the returns.

One day, I found an empty Coke bottle in the back.

"GREAT!" I thought. "Now I'll have an excuse for exploring the cellar. Mommy can't be angry with me if I put an empty where it belongs. Can she?"

Still... I didn't want them to notice me, so I rushed through the store.

I TRIPPED BEFORE REACHING THE CELLAR DOOR!

CRASH!

GLASS, BLOOD— everywhere. My face and arms were covered in cuts.

"OY GEVALT!" shrieks Mommy.

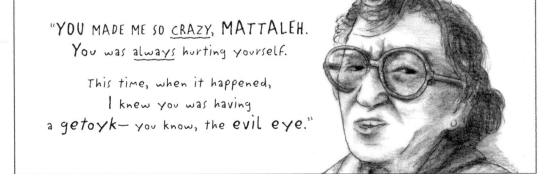

"YOU MADE ME SO <u>CRAZY</u>, MATTALEH. You was <u>always</u> hurting yourself.

This time, when it happened, I knew you was having a *getoyk*— you know, the *evil eye*."

Deh Mameh and I rushed to the toilet...
She sat on the tub until I let loose
with a MIGHTY STREAM.

(You should know, full bladders
are a must for battles
with the Evil Eye.)

Mommy caught some
of my **pee** and
smeared it on my forehead.

Then she twirled me
around and around
as we uttered the INCANTATION,
"Pooh, Pooh, Pooh."

That's how
my MOMMY
conquered
THE EVIL EYE.

P.S.— I never
did get down
to the cellar.

Deh Mameh grew up in a town
where MAGIC was part of the landscape.

Without a doubt,
SPIRITS, GOBLINS, and IMPS
prowled the streets of Germakivka.

They brought about destruction, chaos, disorder.

Oy, what *tsorris*, what *problems*!

"Mattaleh, YOU LAUGH FROM ME always.
Such a *chochum*! Such a *smart alex*!
YOU THINK YOU KNOW <u>EVERYTHING</u>.

"But, some things
you don't understand,
Mr. Bigshot.
Some things
you can't
understand."

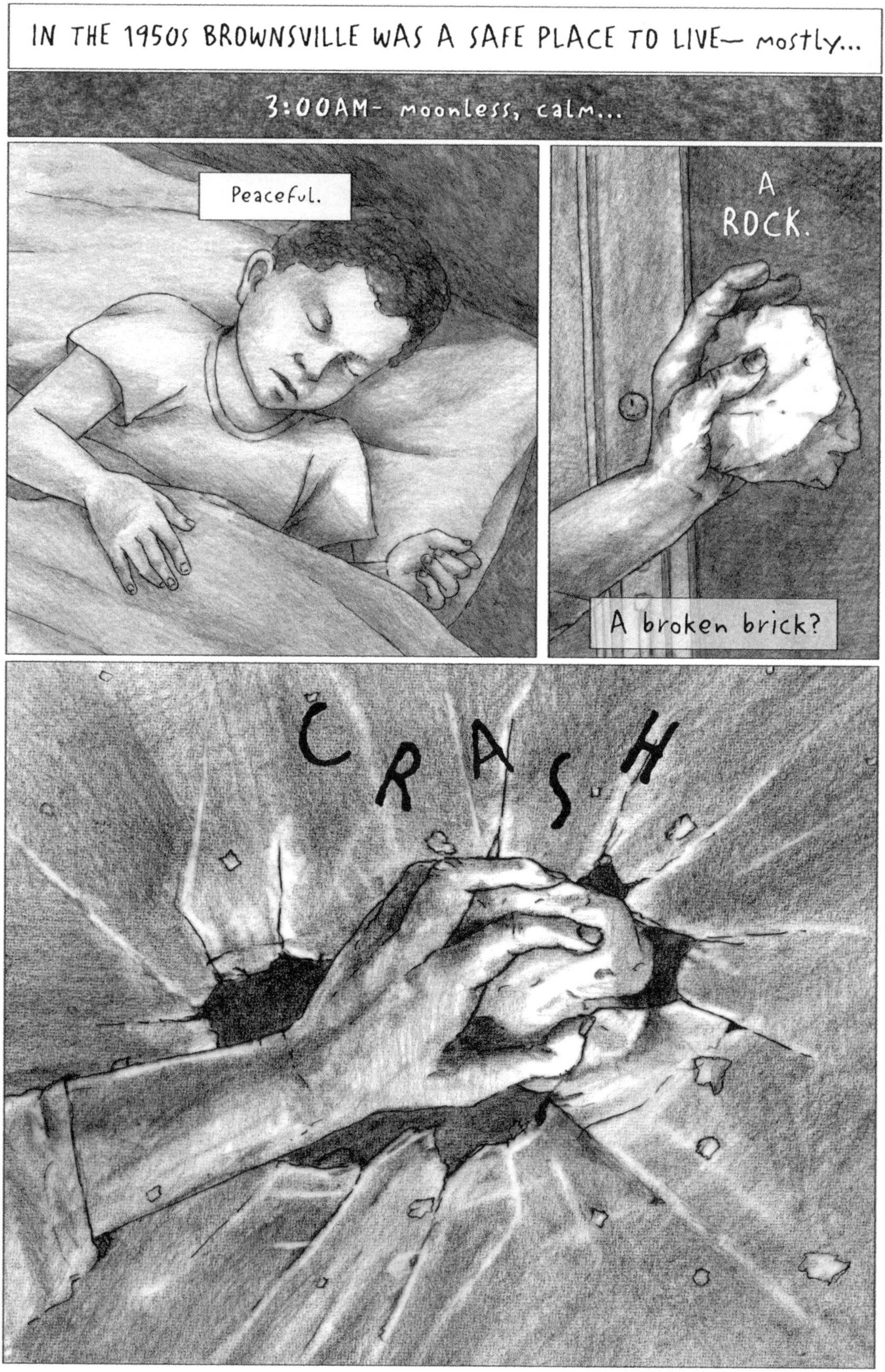
IN THE 1950s BROWNSVILLE WAS A SAFE PLACE TO LIVE— mostly...
3:00AM- moonless, calm...
Peaceful.
A ROCK.
A broken brick?
CRASH

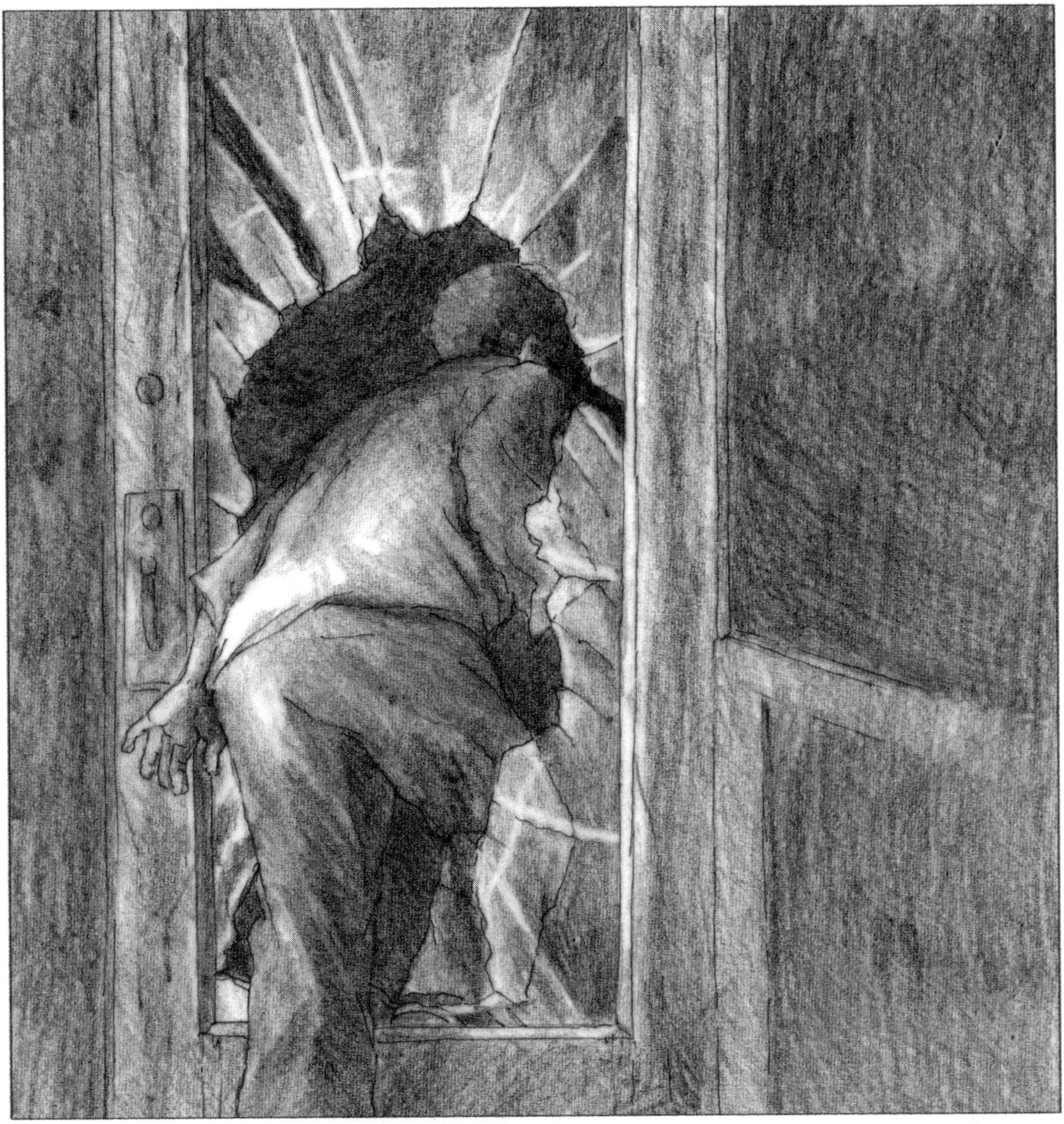

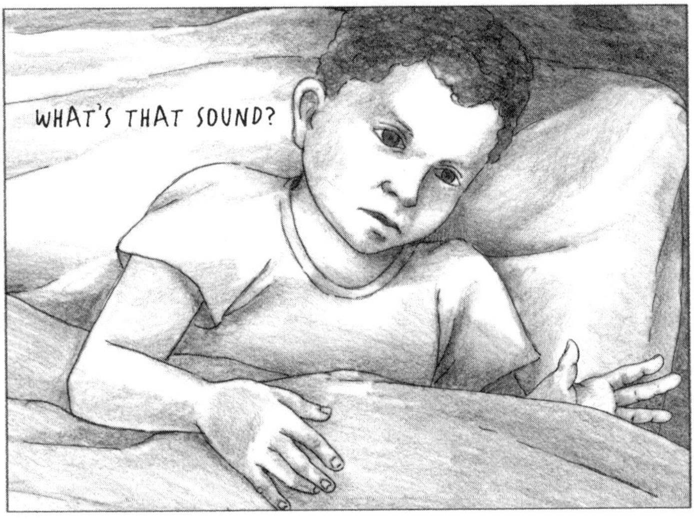
WHAT'S THAT SOUND?

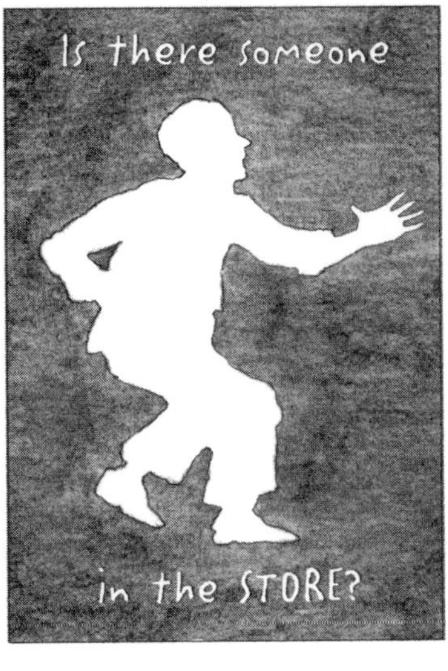
Is there someone
in the STORE?

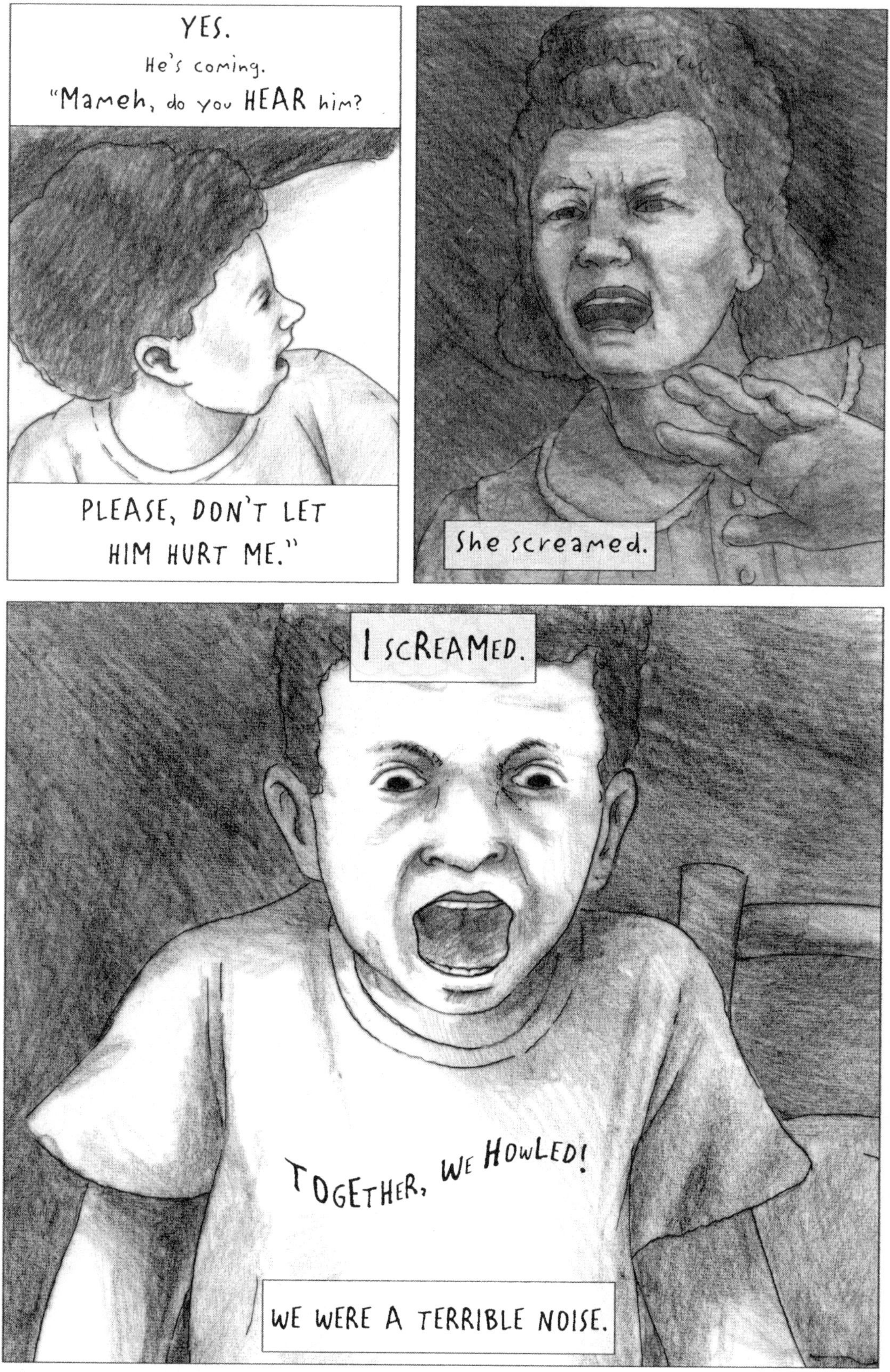
YES.
He's coming.
"Mameh, do you HEAR him?
PLEASE, DON'T LET HIM HURT ME."
She screamed.
I SCREAMED.
TOGETHER, WE HOWLED!
WE WERE A TERRIBLE NOISE.

But look, here's our intruder,
our would-be robber—
a drunk,
a bum,
a *SHLIMAZEL,*
A MAN WITHOUT LUCK.

Instead of breaking into
an empty candy store,

THIS MAN BROKE INTO
OUR HOME.

HE ALSO STUMBLED
INTO MY FATHER.

This is one of the few times in my life,
I was happy to have such an angry FATHER.

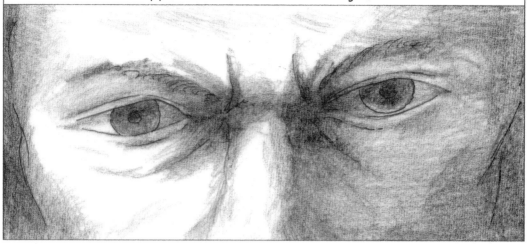

Without a pause, *de Tateh*
punched, kicked, scratched,
choked, whacked, banged,
slapped, and beat
our INTRUDER.

Blood ran
from this SHLIMAZEL'S
nose and mouth.
A tooth fell
on the linoleum.

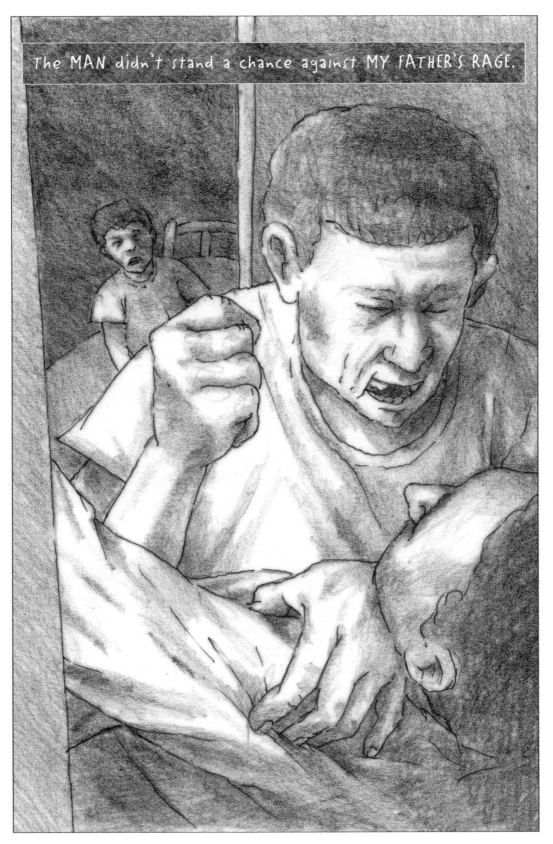

The MAN didn't stand a chance against MY FATHER'S RAGE.

"In the end, your father forced the paskudnyak into the toilet," my mother says.

This schlimiel definitely learned never to mess with MY FATHER'S STORE.

Here he is— crumpled up in our tub.

An hour later the POLICE came and took him away.
("I slept through the whole mess," my brother Bernard says.)

·GRASS-EATERS and the WONDER RABBI·

Es ken nisht shatn.
It can't hurt.
Yiddish saying

"...GRASS-EATERS simply accept the payoffs that the happenstances of police work throw their way."

KNAPP REPORT
Commission to Investigate
Alleged Police Corruption

Chairman Whitman Knapp

The policemen on the Brownsville beat, week in, week out, year in, year out came into the store and grabbed what they wanted— sometimes toys, mostly sodas, always newspapers.

"Mattaleh, we didn't want no tzuris from them."

"Hi, Teddy, my man."

The cop was at our ice box in a flash—
Out came a couple of dripping soda bottles.

HE VANISHED AS QUICKLY AS HE APPEARED, HIS "PURCHASES" CRADLED UNDER HIS ARMS.

"I'm telling you," MOMMY says, "in that time, we all believed, the law was that a POLICEMAN was allowed to take ANYTHING from the stores in the neighborhood."

THE LANDSLEIT

"THE POLICE took from me 2-3 hotdogs a couple times a week— so what. Hey, this don't HURT so much."

"Did you know the Police don't like the Fish? They come to me maybe once a week— on Fridays."

"What is by you, is not by me," says the Fruit Man, "By me, everyday they come. I'm a poor man. Even the few lousy fruits they take hurts me. I want to make a living. They don't let."

Just about then, Stacy came in for his smokes.

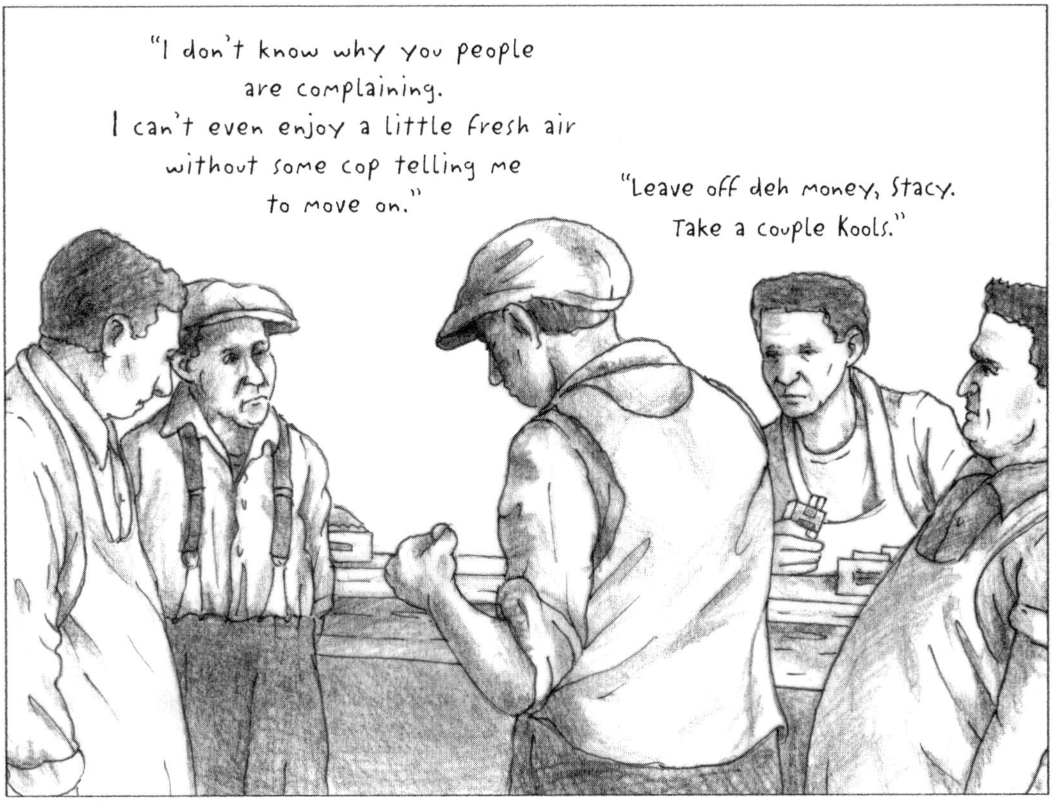
"I don't know why you people are complaining. I can't even enjoy a little fresh air without some cop telling me to move on."
"Leave off deh money, Stacy. Take a couple Kools."

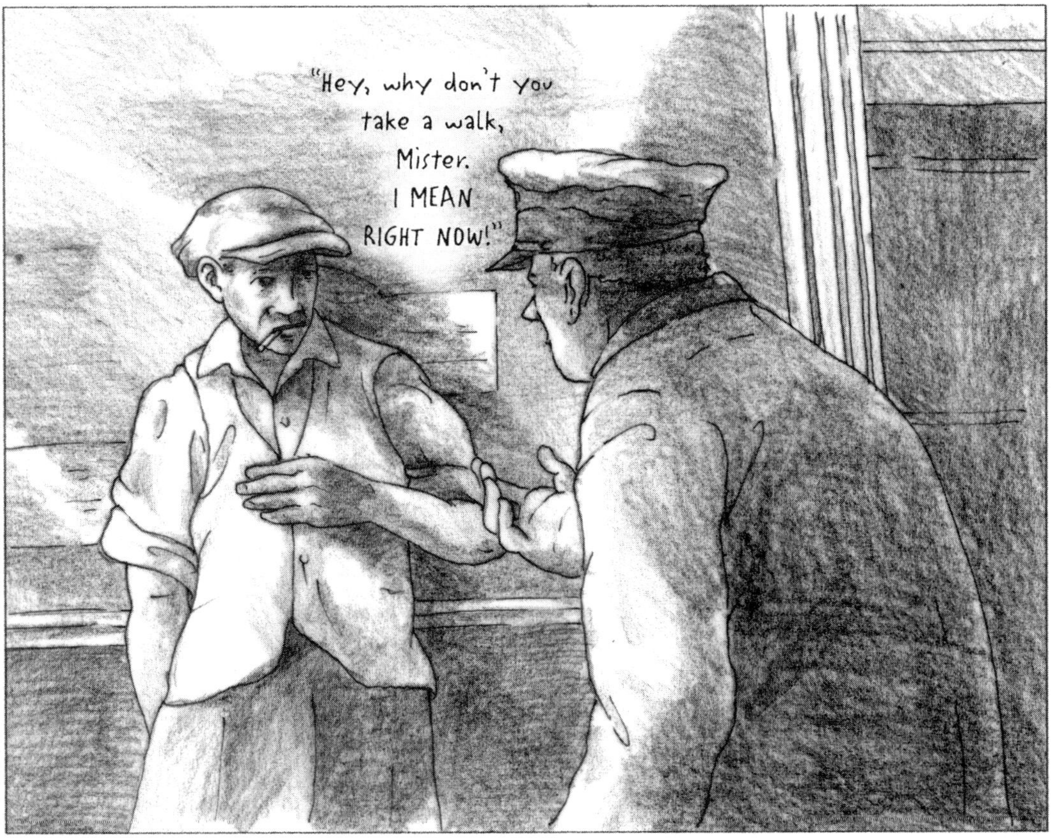
"Hey, why don't you take a walk, Mister. I MEAN RIGHT NOW!"

"From the Police, you don't get no protection.
From God, is the protection.
Listen— you will understand.
This story is from TV and wrestling and a holy man..."

DID YOU KNOW WE DIDN'T PAY NOTHING FOR OUR TV?
The Dairy Crest Company said to your father
'Teddy, you scooped more ice cream
than anyone else, so here,
take a TV for free, for a prize!'

"When they delivered the TV,
I was thinking, 'This will be a
nice surprise for Boynat
and Mattaleh.'"

Mommy turned it on
and went back to work.

That day you couldn't
pry me away
from that thing.

I was hypnotized.

My first show— public affairs.

I DIDN'T UNDERSTAND A WORD
THE MAN WAS SAYING.

But, you wanna know something—
I DIDN'T CARE!

I WAS WATCHING TV!

"This is how to change channels," **Bernard** tells me. "It's really easy."

After, I never miss THE CISCO KID, THE LONE RANGER,

"Hi yo, Silver, and away..."

"Hey, Seesco."

and RIN TIN TIN.

Rusty

I liked any show that included guns, horses, dogs, and cowboys.

BUT, I SIMPLY <u>LOVED</u> WRESTLING.

My goal was to learn all the holds— the Scissors, the Gorilla Press, the Butterfly, the Full Nelson...

Anything, to defeat my arch-enemy— BERNARD!

"YOU'RE LUCKY," Bernard says.
"You get to watch any show.
BUT ME,
am I allowed to watch
KING KONG on MILLION DOLLAR MOVIE?
OF COURSE NOT!
No way—
not allowed, off limits."

"Ooooh, little Mattaleh is a big scaredy cat. WHAT A CHICKEN!"

"GROWWWWL"

"Oy, Boynat, how can I let you watch this monster movie?
Your little brother don't need more bad dreams."

176

"I felt bad I didn't let **Boynat** watch his program," **Mommy** remembers. "So, I wanted to make it up to him.

'**Boynat**,' I said, 'how about, me and you, we go to the Palace Theater for ah *TRIPLE FEATURE*. HOW YOU LIKE THIS?'"

"YES!"

"I was so excited," says **Bernard**. "One of the features at the PALACE was GODZILLA— which I was DYING to see.

Even before we entered the theater, I smelled the buttered popcorn and cigarette smoke ..."

"THE MOVIE WAS ALL I HOPED IT WOULD BE. THE MONSTER WAS SO REALISTIC AND THE DESTRUCTION AMAZING. I DIDN'T EVEN MIND THE GUM STICKING TO MY SHOES."

"IT WAS NICE TO SEE BOYNAT SO HAPPY, BUT I'M THINKING, 'THIS IS THE *DREK* HE LIKES? OY, VEY IZ MIR...'"

Once Bernard and I desperately wanted to watch wrestling on channel 9.
Sad to say, it was past our bedtime...

Deh mameh waited to speak to us separately.

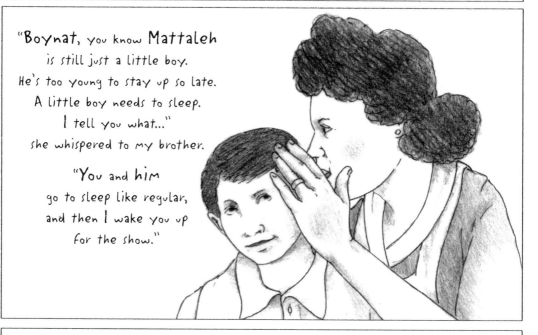

"Boynat, you know Mattaleh
is still just a little boy.
He's too young to stay up so late.
A little boy needs to sleep.
I tell you what..."
she whispered to my brother.

"You and him
go to sleep like regular,
and then I wake you up
for the show."

"Mattaleh, you know Boynat
goes to school.
He needs to wake up early to go.
10 o'clock is too late for him.
I tell you what..."
she whispered to me.

"You and him
go to sleep like regular
and then I wake you up
for the show."

We went to sleep "like regular" and guess what— SHE NEVER WOKE EITHER OF US UP.

It was easy for Mommy to trick us, but much harder to pull a fast one on _her_.

Bernard and I loved to fight, but we had to be very careful where our matches were held.

MOMMY and DADDY's bed was, for obvious reasons, off limits, and B's bed was very dangerous— too near the fridge.

MY BED WAS _JUST_ RIGHT.

"That day," remembers Bernard, "I didn't know my own strength. I felt like Killer Kowalski. NO—I _WAS_ KILLER KOWALSKI."

The battle started out as usual— Bernard got me in a full nelson. Then I wriggled out. He body-scissored me and then my head-butt knocked the air out of him. I kicked him in the ass for good measure. YES!

"So then I decided to finish you off, Martin. NO MORE MISTER NICE GUY."

He plucked me off the mattress and, with all his might, THREW ME AGAINST THE WALL.

"Aieeeeeeeeel!...."

CRASH!

CRASH!

CRACK!

"AARGH, what a hole you made, Martin!" he said, horrified at the mess.

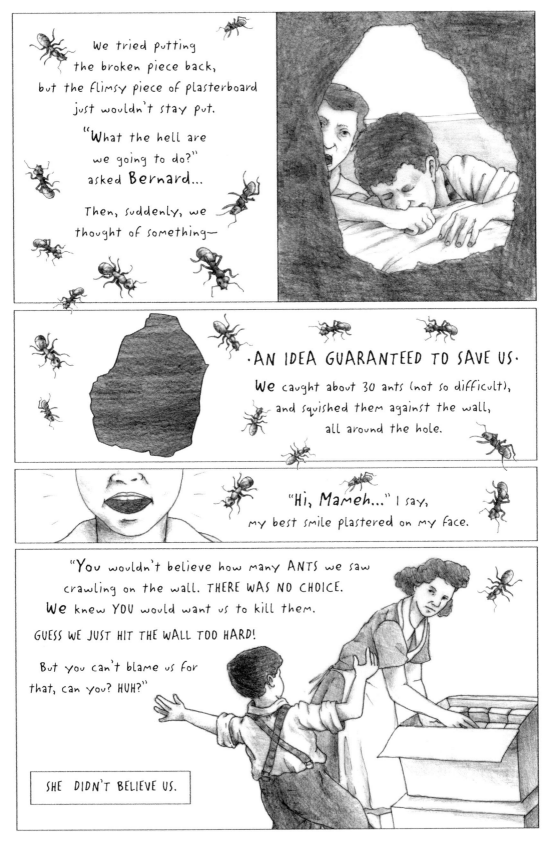

We tried putting the broken piece back, but the flimsy piece of plasterboard just wouldn't stay put.

"What the hell are we going to do?" asked Bernard...

Then, suddenly, we thought of something—

·AN IDEA GUARANTEED TO SAVE US·

We caught about 30 ants (not so difficult), and squished them against the wall, all around the hole.

"Hi, Mameh..." I say, my best smile plastered on my face.

"You wouldn't believe how many ANTS we saw crawling on the wall. THERE WAS NO CHOICE. We knew YOU would want us to kill them. GUESS WE JUST HIT THE WALL TOO HARD!

But you can't blame us for that, can you? HUH?"

SHE DIDN'T BELIEVE US.

"Mattaleh.
What do you think,
I was
born yesterday?"
says Mommy.

"You and Boynat
don't give me
no peace."

For many years,
I slept next to
that hole in the wall.

We never told
Mr. Weselowsky,
our janitor.

"What troubles
if he would find out,"
says Mommy.

"Oy MATTLALEH, MATTLALEH,
I didn't know what
to do with you.
And the FATHER was no help."

"My son is making me the grey hairs," Mommy tells her best friend Etel. "ALWAYS HE HURTS HIMSELF! If it's not his head, it's the foot. If it's not the foot, it's a hand.

"I want him to live so I can see him covered by the chupah at his marriage."

"Plain and simple," says Etel, "this boy has the EVIL EYE.

You need to go to talk to the GREAT RABBI MEIR.

I'm not ashamed to say he helped me many times with a *Getoyk* like this."

And so on a Tuesday during *Sukkos*, the Festival of Booths, Mommy and I traveled to Flatbush to visit Etel's Miracle Man.

"Say hello, Mattaleh."

The Miracle Rabbi,
a gentle looking man,
seemed to know that I was curious
about his house.

"Gey, kindele," he says.
He lets me explore...

THE RABBI'S HOUSE WAS A WONDER.

I walked on rugs, not linoleum.
There was a staircase— just like
on Father Knows Best.
"He must sleep upstairs," I think.

Then... I spot a SUKKAH*.

I crawled out an
open window
to get into it.

IT WAS BEAUTIFUL!

Decorations hung
from the roof.

It smelled
of apples
and citron.

There was a
lulav and essrog
on the table.

*A sukkah is a temporary hut built in memory of the shelters
used by Jews as they wandered the desert after their escape from Egypt.

I played, while **deh Mameh** told the **Rabbi** all of our *tsuris*, our troubles.

The **Sukkah** was my fort in the Wild West— I was surrounded by Indians eager for my scalp. Of course, I bravely fought them off.

After a while, **Mommy** calls me in.

The **Rabbi** laid his hands on my head and blessed me. "**God** willing, live a long and healthy life."

After, he gave me an AMULET— guaranteed to keep me SAFE.

The Charm was made of red construction paper.

The Hebrew letter *SHIN* was inscribed on the front in ballpoint pen. A strip of Scotch tape covered it.

I felt something hard inside, but was afraid to open it.

I didn't want to spoil MY GOOD LUCK.

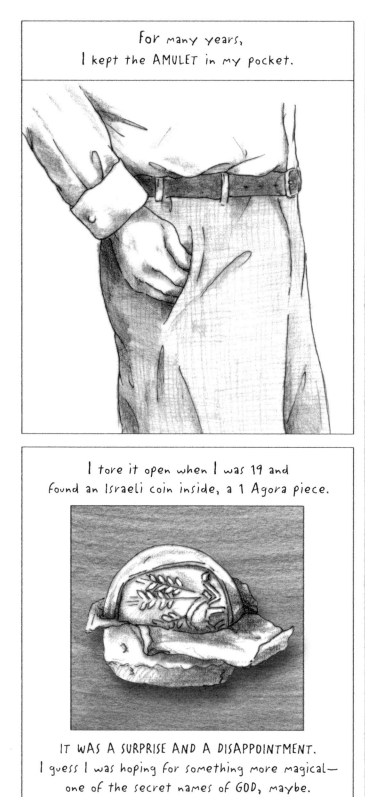

For many years,
I kept the AMULET in my pocket.

I tore it open when I was 19 and
found an Israeli coin inside, a 1 Agora piece.

IT WAS A SURPRISE AND A DISAPPOINTMENT.
I guess I was hoping for something more magical—
one of the secret names of GOD, maybe.

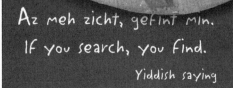

Az meh zicht, gefint men.
If you search, you find.

Yiddish saying

When I was younger I believed that the Amulet _was_ MAGIC.
With it, tucked deep in my pocket, I felt invincible— I ALSO FELT LUCKY.

One day, not long after our trip to the Wonder Rabbi, I decided
to explore the shelves and drawers that lined the walls of the store.
They held some old merchandise and junk from the previous candy store.
It was stuff Mommy and Daddy didn't think they could sell—

"It's drek, Mattaleh," they told me.
I WAS CONVINCED I'D DISCOVER TREASURE.

I found dustballs, a case of dried inkbottles, lumpy tubes of glue, cracked toys...

I unearthed packs and packs of HOME RUN cigarettes in a compartment near
the telephones— They were old, forgotten, not a brand Daddy could sell.
I opened a pack. The cigarettes inside smelled sweet,
like honey.

"One day," I think,
"I'll smoke one.
Hmmm...
I'll smoke
quite a few,
in fact!"

And then, paydirt! I uncovered brushes, cakes of watercolor, and oil paints—part of an incomplete Paint-By-Number set. I found enamel model airplane paints and a large cache of school tempera paints. There was a wooden palette.

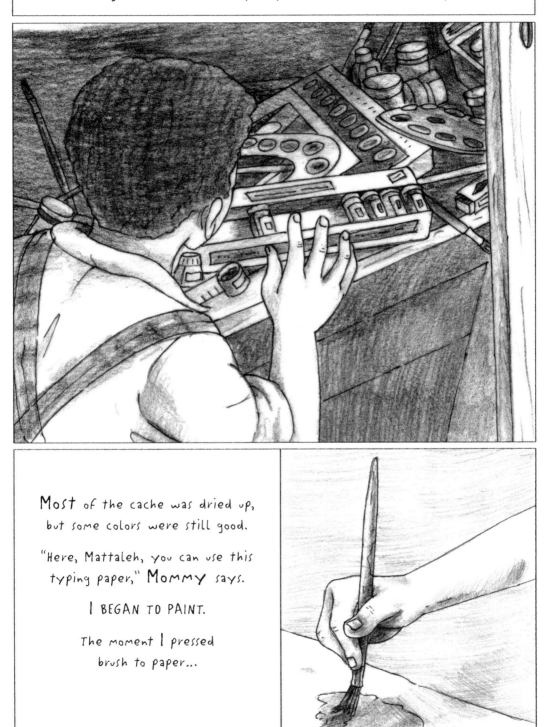

Most of the cache was dried up, but some colors were still good.

"Here, Mattaleh, you can use this typing paper," Mommy says.

I BEGAN TO PAINT.

The moment I pressed brush to paper...

TIME SLOWED DOWN. MINUTES TURNED INTO HOURS. As if by magic—
a face appeared on my paper, a tree, a house, a bird, a Pepsi bottle, hands...

The cracked walls, dusty floors, screaming parents, worries, faded away.
All I saw and felt were the marks I made on the paper.

I DREW AND
PAINTED IN A FRENZY.

I was a painting machine,
finishing dozens
of pieces a day—
on the typewriter paper
Mommy gave me,
on scrap cardboard
I tore from old boxes.
The airplane glue made
me dizzy.

The floors were papered
with drying art.

"Boy, Martin, how'd you paint that tree?" Bernard says. "It almost looks real."

MY BROTHER THOUGHT I WAS A GENIUS! MOMMY THOUGHT I WAS CRAZY.

"Oy, Mattaleh, why you need to waste your time? For what you need all this PAINTING BUSINESS?"
"I like it, Mameh. Aren't the pictures beautiful?"
"FEH."

She didn't like what I was doing. Still she had advice for me—
"Mattaleh, if you want to make a nice picture, don't finish in a day. Take your time. IT WILL BE BETTER."

GOOD ADVICE.

In fact, I've been following that tip for 50 years.

191

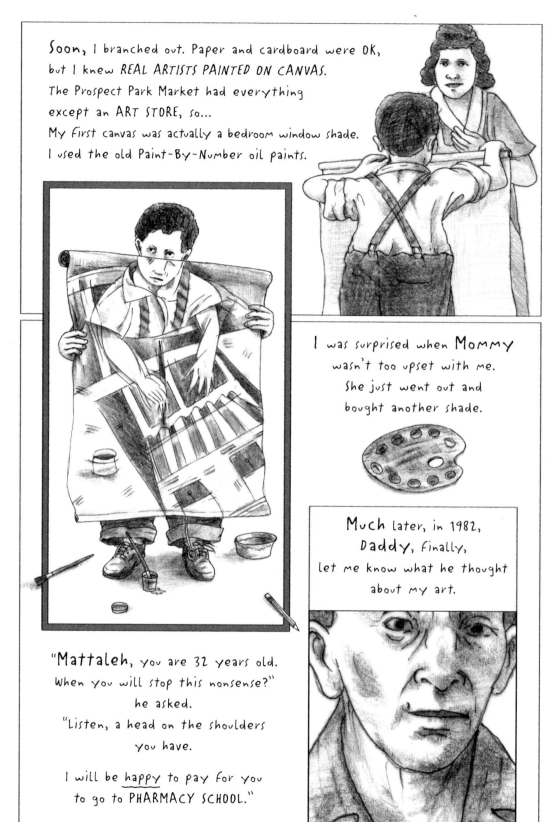

Soon, I branched out. Paper and cardboard were OK, but I knew REAL ARTISTS PAINTED ON CANVAS. The Prospect Park Market had everything except an ART STORE, so...
My first canvas was actually a bedroom window shade.
I used the old Paint-By-Number oil paints.

I was surprised when MOMMY wasn't too upset with me. She just went out and bought another shade.

Much later, in 1982, Daddy, finally, let me know what he thought about my art.

"Mattaleh, you are 32 years old. When you will stop this nonsense?" he asked.
"Listen, a head on the shoulders you have.

I will be happy to pay for you to go to PHARMACY SCHOOL."

Di bowch farshlingt di kop miten seichel.
The stomach swallows the brains.

Yiddish saying

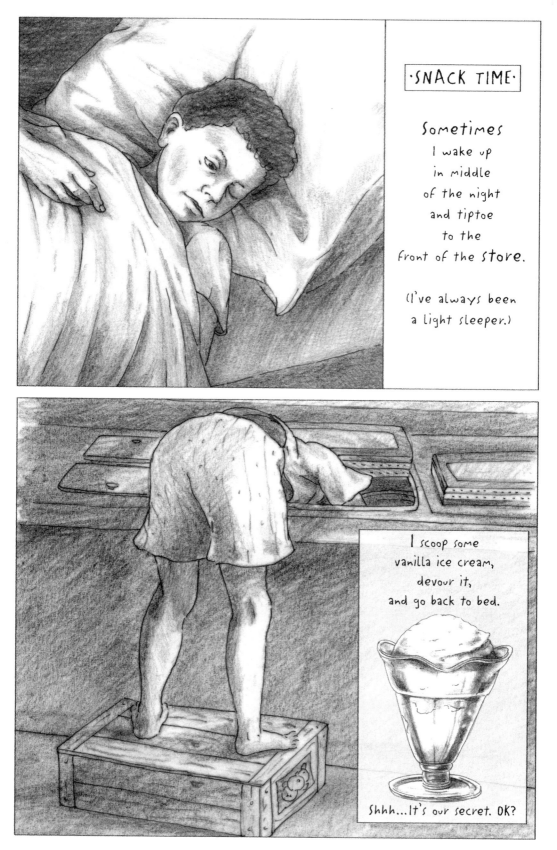

·SNACK TIME·

Sometimes
I wake up
in middle
of the night
and tiptoe
to the
front of the store.

(I've always been
a light sleeper.)

I scoop some
vanilla ice cream,
devour it,
and go back to bed.

Shhh...It's our secret. OK?

MORNING

7:00ᴀᴍ—TIME TO GET UP.

I was still in
my underwear,
when I walked
past the furniture
and merchandise—
'Hmm, I wonder what's
going on in the FRONT?'

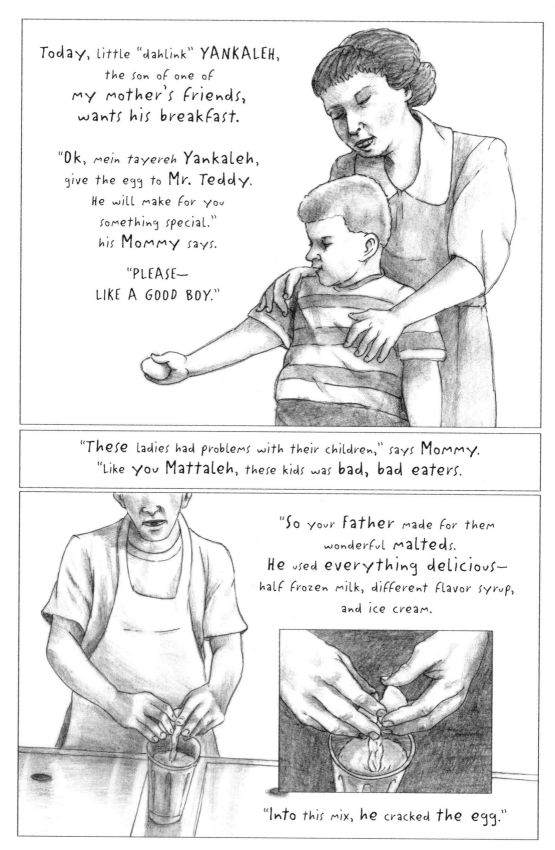

Today, little "dahlink" YANKALEH, the son of one of my mother's friends, wants his breakfast.

"Ok, mein tayereh Yankaleh, give the egg to Mr. Teddy. He will make for you something special." his Mommy says.

"PLEASE— LIKE A GOOD BOY."

"These ladies had problems with their children," says Mommy. "Like you Mattaleh, these kids was bad, bad eaters.

"So your father made for them wonderful malteds. He used everything delicious— half frozen milk, different flavor syrup, and ice cream.

"Into this mix, he cracked the egg."

"After your father finished making the malted, Yankaleh, no, all the children drank and licked the fingers, it was so good.

"This made the mothers so happy—NOURISHMENT FOR THEIR BABIES!"

My brother, Bernard, and I weren't so lucky.

Oy vey, to think what we had to eat for breakfast.

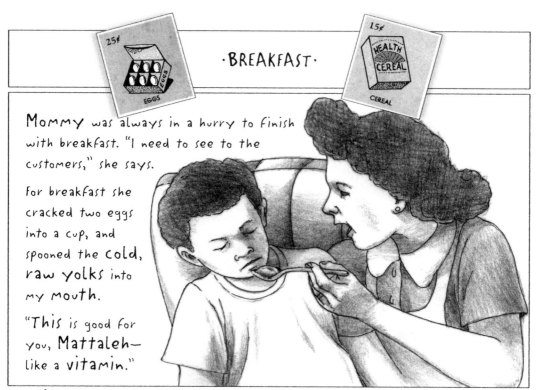

Mommy was always in a hurry to finish with breakfast. "I need to see to the customers," she says.

For breakfast she cracked two eggs into a cup, and spooned the cold, raw yolks into my mouth.

"This is good for you, Mattaleh— like a vitamin."

As we grew older, Bernard and I made our own food. We couldn't stand the slimy taste of raw yolks so early in the morning.

"MATTALEH! MATTALEH! You don't know from what you are talking about!" Mommy says.

"What kind of a baba maisa is this? I cooked for the family! I made you food and it was delicious.

For breakfast I cooked sometimes grishig, porridge, sometimes kasha with milk, sometimes oatmeal.

WHAT, YOU DON'T REMEMBER THIS?"

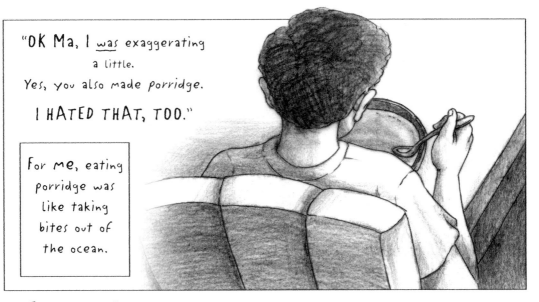

"OK Ma, I _was_ exaggerating a little.
Yes, you also made porridge.
I HATED THAT, TOO."

For me, eating porridge was like taking bites out of the ocean.

Every time I scooped a spoonful into my mouth, the food in the bowl just smoothed itself back out— VERY FRUSTRATING. I preferred to see actual progress when I ate...

"Mattaleh, you need to make for yourself a head examination. YOU ARE REALLY CRAZY!

You make such a problem.

I tell you plain, you don't like to eat good food.
You even don't know what is good food."

"Mattaleh, have some rachmunis on me.

You _know_ I didn't have so much time to make the food.

You _know_ your father needed me in the store."

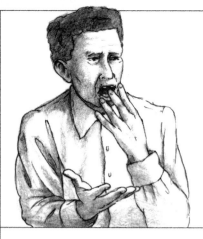

"WHO NEEDS YOU LADY!
Goddamn—
I need you in the store
like I need a <u>cholera</u>,
like I need a <u>cancer</u>..."

"ACH— YOU HAVE SO MUCH KAS FOR ME, TOVIA.
What— did I force you to work in the store?
Did I force you to come to Brooklyn— to America.

Do you think all I want from this life
is to <u>trick</u> you,
to make a fool from you?"

Mommy and Daddy fought every day.
I never knew when they were going to start.
A look, or a gesture, or sometimes absolutely nothing
was enough to start the yelling. It was always...
"You ruined my life." "No, you ruined my life."
"Your rotten family." "You drunk." On and on and on.

"I wanted HE should appreciate
my help in the store."
HE DIDN'T.

"I wanted SHE should understand
how clever I am."
SHE DIDN'T.

"I wanted HE should appreciate
how I bring up the children."
HE DIDN'T.

"I wanted SHE should respect me."
SHE DIDN'T.

My Mother and Father fight about everything, anything.

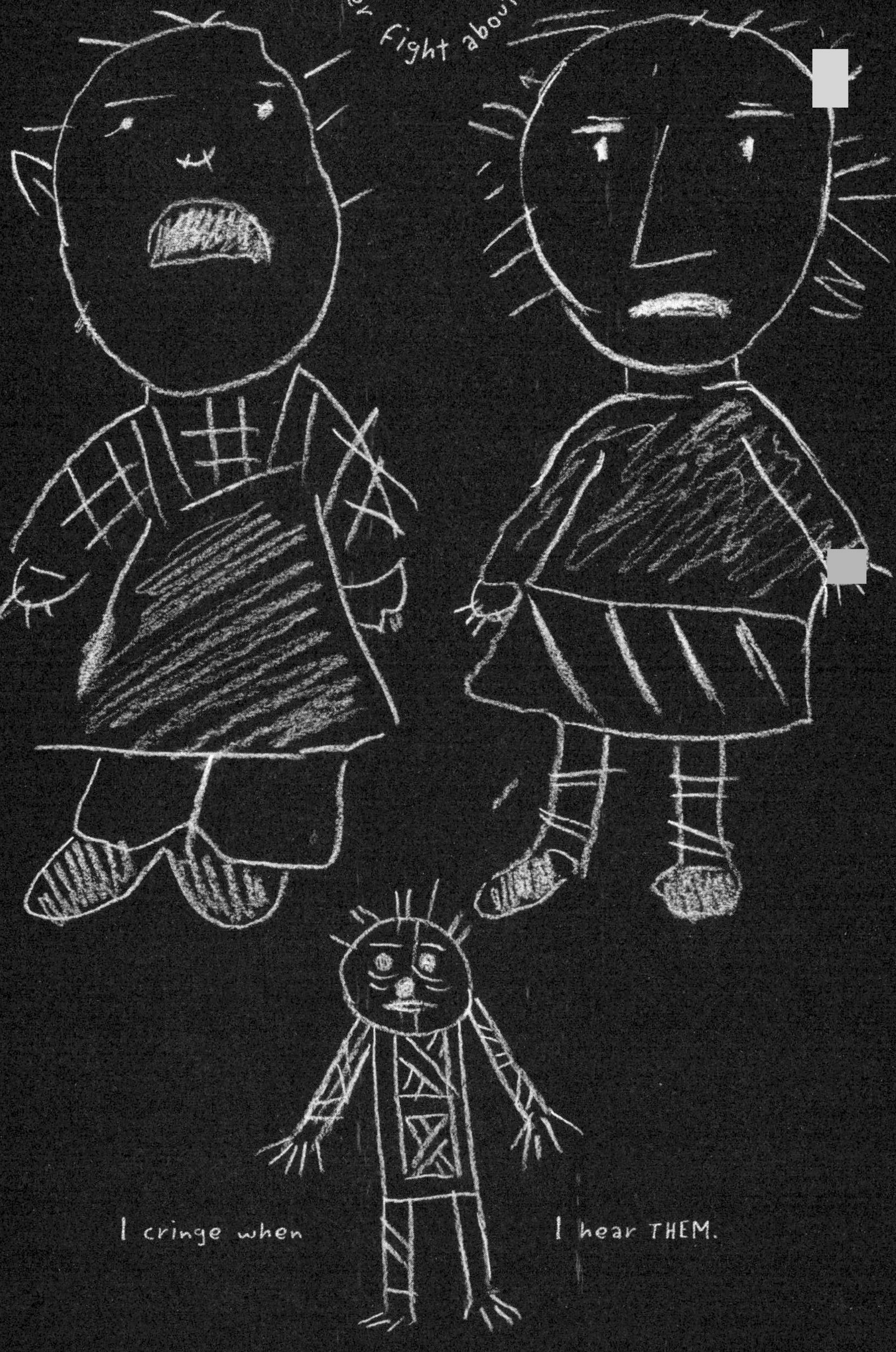

I cringe when I hear THEM.

My father ate very little.

His anger fed him. His rage filled him up.

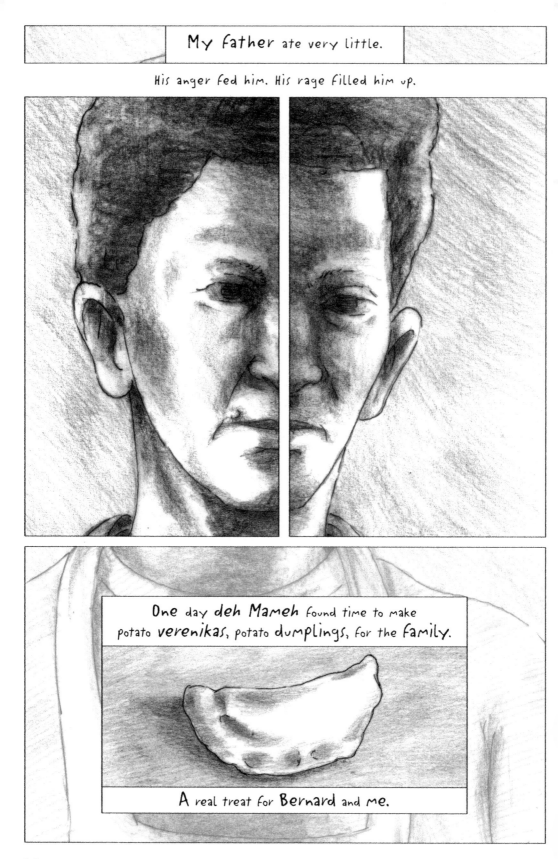

One day deh Mameh found time to make potato **verenikas**, potato **dumplings**, for the **family**.

A real treat for **Bernard** and me.

She wanted Daddy to have some for lunch.
He'd eat them behind the counter.

Steam rose from the bowl. What a delicious smell!

"*Nem shoin avek*, take it away now," my father growled at her.
"This, I don't want."

Mommy would not take NO for an answer.
HE HAD TO LIKE HER COOKING.
His refusal was a personal insult.

"How could you not want. I make so TASTY.
EAT, EAT, EAT, EAT, EAT, EAT, EAT, EAT!"

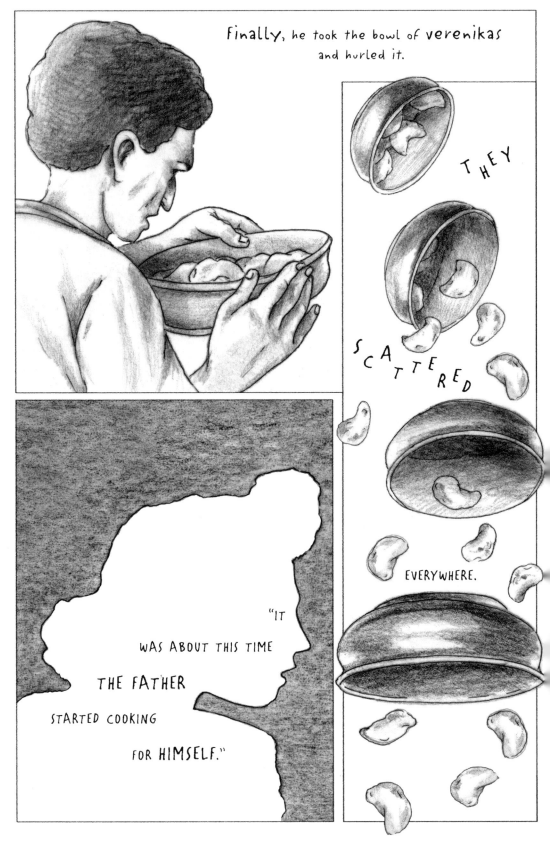

Finally, he took the bowl of **verenikas** and hurled it.

THEY

SCATTERED

EVERYWHERE.

"IT WAS ABOUT THIS TIME THE FATHER STARTED COOKING FOR HIMSELF."

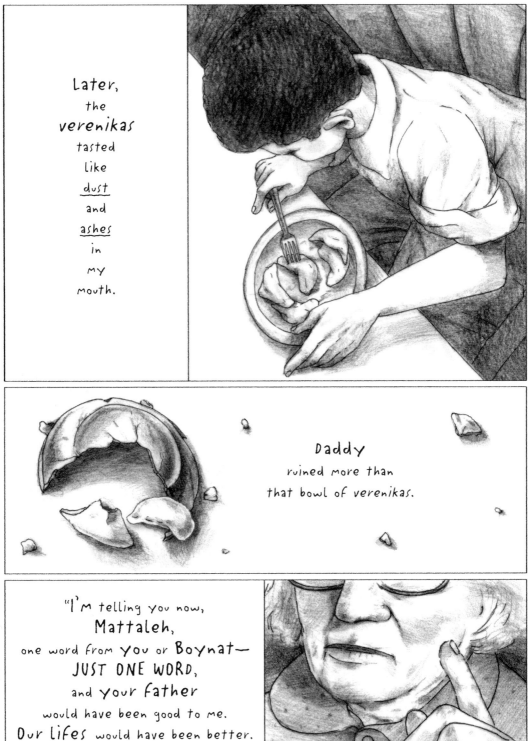

Later,
the
verenikas
tasted
like
<u>dust</u>
and
<u>ashes</u>
in
my
mouth.

Daddy
ruined more than
that bowl of verenikas.

"I'm telling you now,
Mattaleh,
one word from **you** or **Boynat—**
JUST ONE WORD,
and **your father**
would have been good to me.
Our lifes would have been better.

Why YOU BOYS couldn't help me,
I don't know."

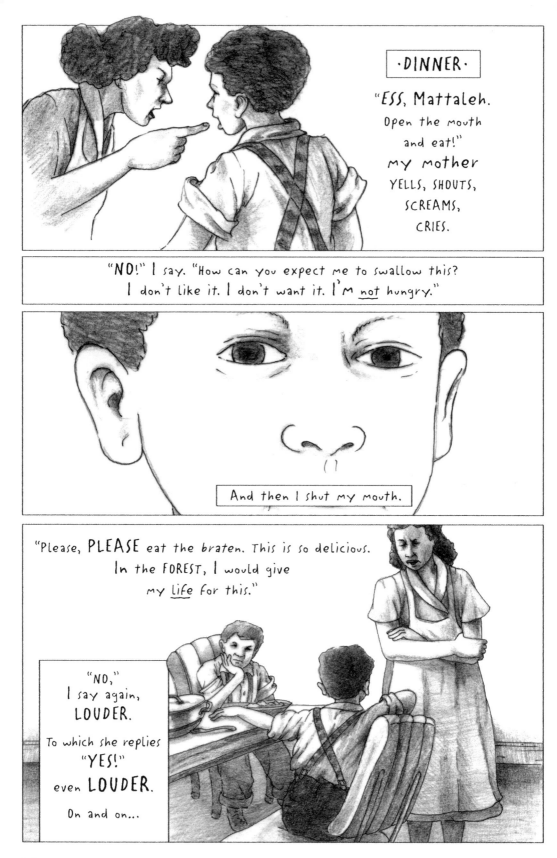

· DINNER ·

"*ESS*, Mattaleh.
Open the mouth
and eat!"
MY MOTHER
YELLS, SHOUTS,
SCREAMS,
CRIES.

"NO!" I say. "How can you expect me to swallow this?
I don't like it. I don't want it. I'M <u>not</u> hungry."

And then I shut my mouth.

"Please, PLEASE eat the braten. This is so delicious.
In the FOREST, I would give
my <u>life</u> for this."

"NO,"
I say again,
LOUDER.

To which she replies
"YES!"
even LOUDER.

On and on...

" Why can't You just **EAT** what **she** puts in front of **YOU**?"
my brother says.

"JUST TO KEEP HER **QUIET**...
Why do YOU have to cause more problems for us?"

"I can't help myself, **Bernard**.
I HATE what she makes.

Boiled meat and vegetables,
braten— I hate it!
Just for once, why not something
that hasn't been <u>boiled</u>?"

"Oy, **Mattaleh**, how could
I **bake** in back from the store?
The oven is broken.
The **rats** lived inside."

And, when I _did_ eat, Mommy couldn't stand the way I trimmed the fat off of my meat— how I separated the "good stuff" from the "bad."

"Why do you cut so much?" she says. "You throw everything away."

(After my "surgery," I have to admit, a six ounce piece of meat ended up a mere two ounces.)

Bernard couldn't stand the bickering between Mommy and me.

IT DROVE HIM CRAZY.

He wanted peace. He longed for quiet. SOMETIMES, HE HATED ME.

· BERNARD CRACKS UP ·

"STOP FIGHTING WITH MOMMY YOU LITTLE PIG," he shouts.

"EAT, EAT, EAT!"

FINGERS SQUEEZE
MY NECK.

HE WON'T LET GO.

I CAN'T BREATHE.

NOW THERE ARE SPOTS
IN FRONT
OF MY EYES.

"Oh," I think,
"Bernard is
trying
to kill me."

"THEN **MOMMY** STARTED YELLING AT ME," Bernard remembers.
"I COULDN'T BELIEVE IT. SHE WAS TAKING <u>YOUR</u> SIDE!
All I wanted to do was help her get you to **SHUT UP** and eat her <u>damn</u> food."

But, did I hate my brother
for trying to
MURDER ME?

On the contrary.
In the 1950s and 1960s,
he was my island of sanity.
If I had a problem,
I went to him.

"Hey, **Martin**,"
says Bernard, "you
should tell them about
the PRETZEL BOX DISASTER."

·THE PRESENT·

Oy, ah gezunt dir in kepele!
Oy, a blessing on your little head!

Yiddish saying

Scattered around our living room were metal tins
filled with 2 CENT PRETZEL RODS— 3 FOR A NICKEL.
Great chairs for me — just my size.
THEY WERE REALLY HEAVY.
I had to slide them across the linoleum floor to move them.

One day, on a whim, I picked one up... just to see how strong I was.

"Oh!"

The TIN slipped and
DROPPED on MY BIG TOE.

AGONIZING PAIN! SEARING PAIN!

I wanted to cry out.

BUT,
I DIDN'T.

I
knew
that if
Mommy
heard
me,
she'd
become
hysterical.

At that moment, I didn't have the strength to BEAR MY PAIN and COMFORT HER, TOO.

I KNEW, WITHOUT A DOUBT, THAT I'D END UP TRYING TO CONVINCE HER I WAS OK— THAT I WASN'T DYING.

I TOLD BERNARD INSTEAD.

"Mattaleh, how could I not be hysterical? MY whole life I feel MEIN KERPER ZEET TUMID, MY BODY IS ALWAYS BOILING.

ALWAYS, it is the same. There is not a moment I feel I deserve to have PEACE."

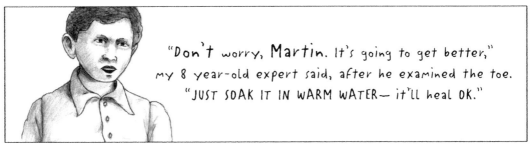

"Don't worry, Martin. It's going to get better," my 8 year-old expert said, after he examined the toe. "JUST SOAK IT IN WARM WATER— it'll heal OK."

The water DID feel good on the toe.

But, day by day, my nail got worse. First it turned yellow, then purple, then black.

Mommy began to sense something fishy going on. "Mattaleh," she asks, "why, everyday, you keep washing your feet?" "Mameh, my ankles are dirty," I bluff. "I want to keep them clean. TAKE A LOOK IF YOU WANT."

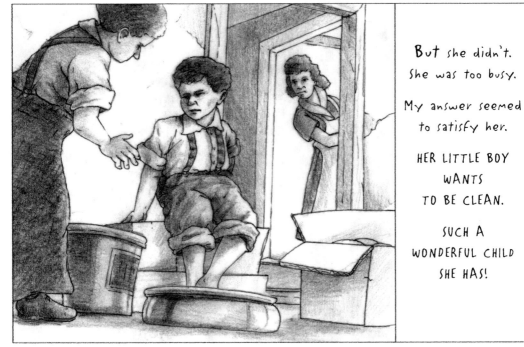

But she didn't. She was too busy.

My answer seemed to satisfy her.

HER LITTLE BOY WANTS TO BE CLEAN.

SUCH A WONDERFUL CHILD SHE HAS!

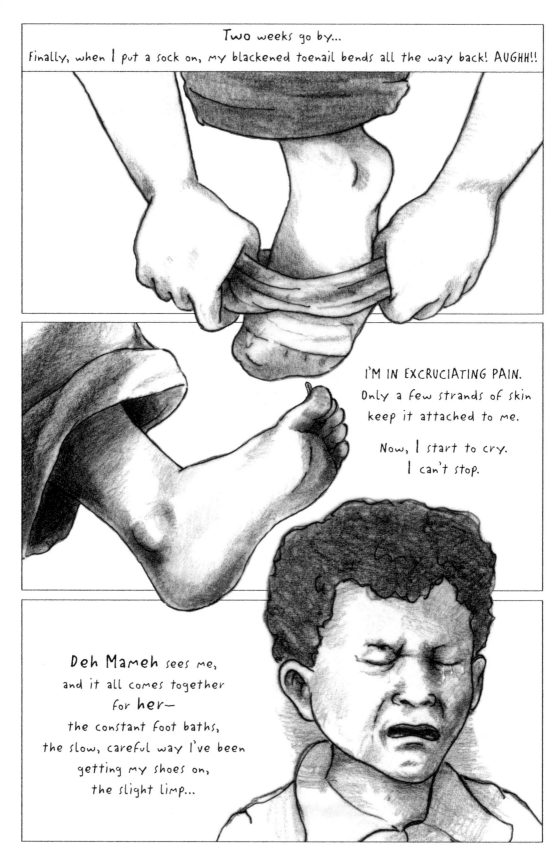

Two weeks go by...
Finally, when I put a sock on, my blackened toenail bends all the way back! AUGHH!!

I'M IN EXCRUCIATING PAIN.
Only a few strands of skin keep it attached to me.

Now, I start to cry.
I can't stop.

Deh Mameh sees me,
and it all comes together
for her—
the constant foot baths,
the slow, careful way I've been
getting my shoes on,
the slight limp...

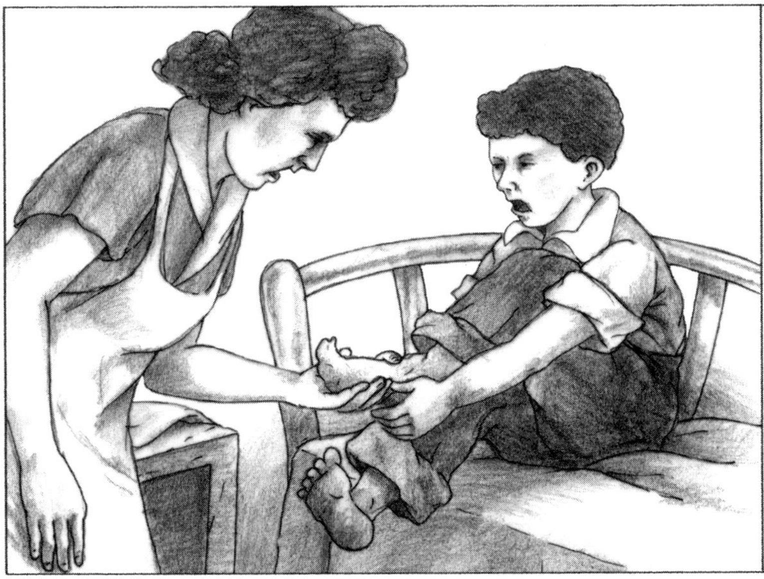

"MATTALEH, MATTALEH, MATTALEH! WHY YOU DIDN'T TELL ME? YOU LOUSY CHILD. I should beat you so hard you wouldn't be able to WALK!"

We took the bus to Herr Doctor Matasoff— my mother yelling at me the whole way there.

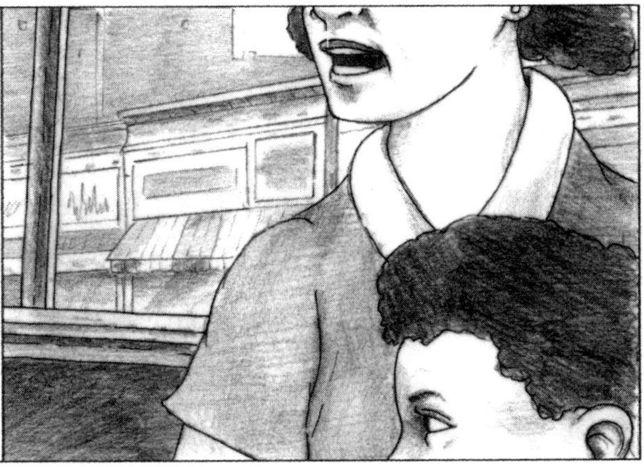

Fortunately, it didn't take the Doctor long to snip off my blackened toenail, and bandage me up. "Don't worry," he says. "You're going to be AS GOOD AS NEW."

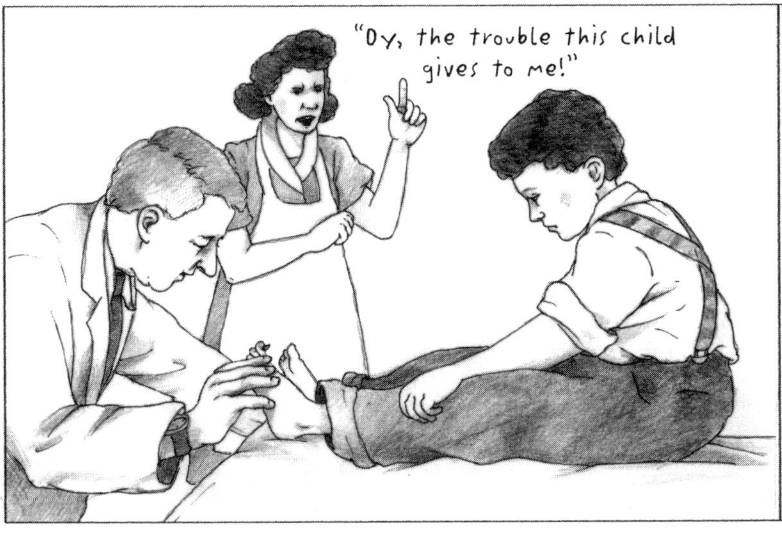
"Oy, the trouble this child gives to me!"

Most of OUR VISIT was taken up by Mommy informing the Herr Doctor what a rat I was.

You have to **believe me** when I tell you that I felt really bad about upsetting **Mommy.**

I WANTED TO MAKE IT UP TO HER.
I DECIDED TO MAKE IT UP TO HER.

SO...

You should know that **my father** never owned a cash register. "**Feh,** who needs such a thing," he says. He kept all the **gelt** in an open metal box near the cigarettes...

When no one was looking, I helped myself to **2 dollars.**

Then, **Bernard** and I crossed Howard Avenue, the gelt tucked deep in my pants pocket.

"**Hey,** where are you guys going?" calls Bernard's best friend, **Benny.**

"WE'RE ON A MISSION, BENNY," I shout up to him. "WE'RE ON A MISSION!"

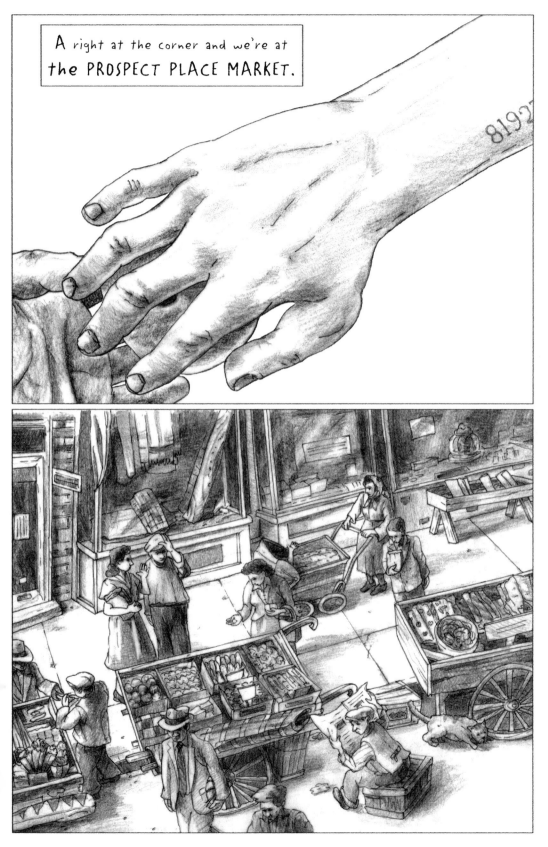

A right at the corner and we're at **the PROSPECT PLACE MARKET.**

There was always something going on at the MARKET—
rushing, yelling, pushing, bargaining, and once in a while, a fist fight.
Life was everywhere.
"Listen, Missus, take a chance. Come in." "Hey, Mister, we got good prices."

PUSHCARTS— wooden wagons, iron wheels, handwritten signs,
hanging merchandise, vegetables, fruit, *KOL MATAMIM, EVERYTHING DELICIOUS.*

As Bernard and I walked past them,
a thought popped into my head—
"I wish MOMMY would, for once,
buy me some cherries."

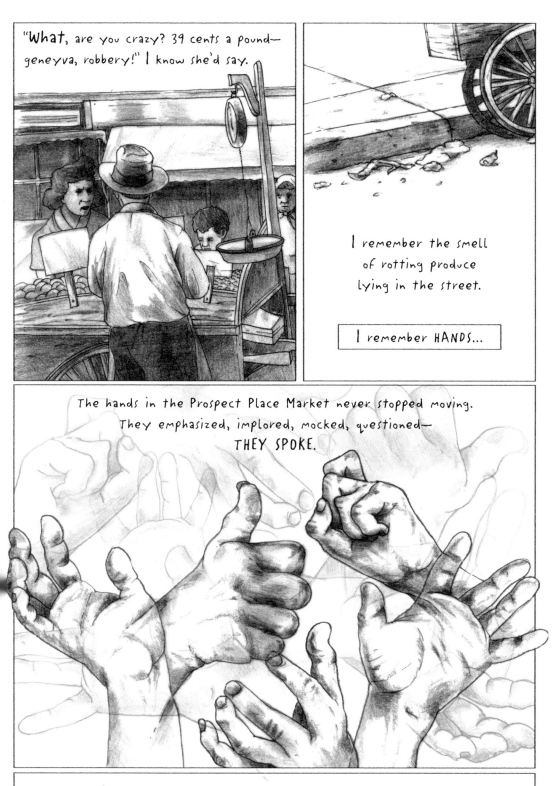

"What, are you crazy? 39 cents a pound—geneyva, robbery!" I know she'd say.

I remember the smell of rotting produce lying in the street.

I remember HANDS...

The hands in the Prospect Place Market never stopped moving. They emphasized, implored, mocked, questioned— THEY SPOKE.

These hands were the same ones that were ripped from the study halls, synagogues, and villages of Eastern Europe.

We had to pass a bunch of stores,
before we got to the one I wanted.

·THE SHOE STORE·

It was a safe bet
that you'd find
the owner,
a tall grey man,
pressed up against
his window,
counting
his change.

I think he hated
being cooped up
inside his store.

Whenever I needed
a pair of shoes
Mommy
took me there.

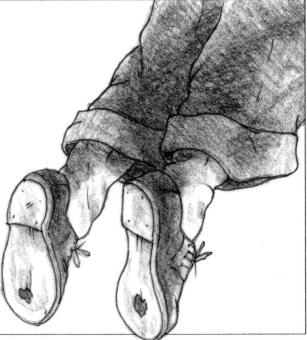

My friend Jan was lucky.
<u>HIS</u> MOTHER took him to
the Thom McAn shoe store
on Pitkin Avenue.

HE EVEN OWNED A PAIR OF SNEAKERS!

All I ever got were
black or brown leather lace-ups.

"You need support, **Mattaleh**, and sneakers don't give you no support," MOMMY says.
"You should never know what is like to have bad feet.
Me, I got frozen feet in the forest. Until this day, they hurt me.

"Please, Mister, give my son
a half size bigger. I want
he should grow into
them."

I hear clucking and squawking. We're passing the KOSHER CHICKEN MARKET.

Inside — hundreds of live, crated **chickens** were waiting their turn to become **kosher.**
Blood-soaked sawdust covered the floor.
The air was hot and wet and smelled of copper and bird shit.

All the balabustas left carrying bags filled with the family's dinner — feathers and feet intact.

"You wouldn't get fresher," they crowed.

If the
Chicken Market
wasn't your cup of tea,
you'd have to walk back
to Howard.
Our neighborhood
Kosher butcher
was right across the street
from Teddy's,
at number 455.

It was much less crowded,
and the man there
sold beef, too.

"This butcher is an honest person," says Mommy.
"He grinds up the chop meat
in front from you.
Sometimes I buy
a steak or flanken from him, too."

The Bakery was two stores down from the Chicken Market.

Its windows were filled with challahs, cookies, cakes, and my favorite, The Charlotte Russe.

"What's a Charlotte Russe?" you ask.

It's sponge cake topped with whipped cream and a maraschino cherry — all in a serrated cardboard container.

Simple...yet beautiful.

Whipped cream

Maraschino cherry

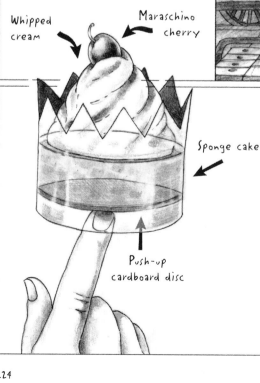

Sponge cake

Push-up cardboard disc

I learned, much later, that the Charlotte Russe I loved was the lowly Brooklyn one.

The original was created for Czar Alexander of Russia.

We hurried past the Barber Shop.

I didn't want the barber to see me.

After each haircut Mommy asks him, "Nu, <u>why</u> I should give a tip?"

I can still remember sitting on that leather booster-seat— the smell of talcum powder, the cold slap of witch hazel on the back of my neck, and those long black combs floating in a jar of blue water.

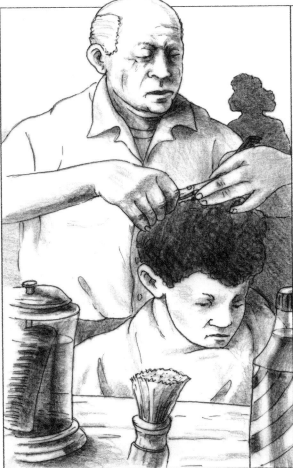

Once,
while shopping
for a winter coat...

"It fits proifect,
Missus,"
says the owner.
"This, I can
guarantee you,
is very stylish."

"How you can charge so much," Mommy says.
"This is robbery, pure geneyvah."

"Missus, I will lose MONEY
if I make cheaper," the owner says.
"This is my lowest price."

"Impossible!
I tell you what—
you throw
something in and I buy
the jacket."

...We left the Clothing store
with my new winter coat
and a bunch of PLASTIC FLOWERS
the owner plucked from his window display.

When we got home, Mommy
puts the flowers on top of our TV—
"to make it nice."

The **Grocery and Appetizing Store** was loaded with
loaves of Moishele's pumpernickel, blocks of Farmer's cheese,
slabs of spongecake, wooden barrels of salty shmaltz herring and dried fruit.

Crammed inside—
Nuts, coffee, candy,
nova lox, smoked sable,
buttermilk, olives...

The tangy smells of
sour pickles and
sour tomatoes
filled my nose.
My mouth watered.

(But, munching on
sour pickles and tomatoes
wasn't why we came.)

"Just what
I'm looking for,"
I tell Bernard.

227

My 2 bucks was more than enough to buy a super-deluxe, heart-shaped, ribbon-wrapped, **box of chocolates.**

(The man gave me 25 cents back.)

I hurried home with my present.

"I'm sorry for hurting my toe, Mameh," I say, as I hand her the BOX.

MOMMY WAS SO SURPRISED.

"In my life, this was one of the best **presents,**" says my mother, still touched.

"That my **Mattaleh** would think on such a thing— this was something."

From then on, **Deh Mameh** kept all her photographs
in my present, that chocolate box.

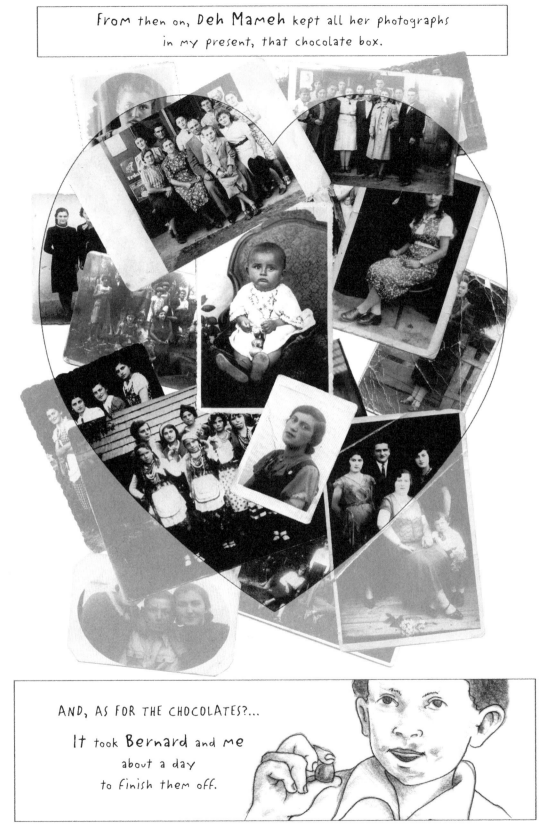

AND, AS FOR THE CHOCOLATES?...

It took **Bernard** and me
about a day
to finish them off.

MATTALEH GOES TO SCHOOL

Toyrah iz de beste schoirah.
Torah is the best merchandise.
Yiddish saying

"I have a hard time when I take the TEST FOR THE CITIZENSHIP," deh Mameh says.

"To answer all the questions, for me, was not so easy.

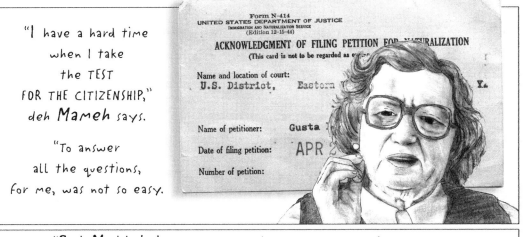

"But Mattaleh, you know, this I tell the man from the test, 'Mister, now I don't <u>know</u> everything, but later, you will see, my children will go to school and THEY WILL TEACH ME.'

"Der Tateh, I don't understand— He didn't give me no problems when I wanted Boynat to go to the Yeshiva. You, Mattaleh, was another story..."

"I am telling you, Gusta, Mattaleh don't need to go to the Yeshiva,"
Daddy says. "What— you want HE should be a Rabbi like Boynat?
THE PUBLIC SCHOOL is on the corner.
We already spend 11 DOLLARS for Boynat's Yeshiva.

"Did you forget
how hard it is
to make 11 dollars
from nickel cones?"

Deh Tateh won the argument.

And so, in September of 1956, I started PUBLIC SCHOOL at 430 Howard.
It was just a short walk from the store, across the street from the pharmacy.

Everything went well, for a little while... But, one morning in late October, a plate smashes into my skull.

"SORRY," the plate-thrower whines, "I wasn't aiming for you."

It hurts. I'm bleeding.

Let's go down to the NURSE and then I'll call your MOMMY.

Oy, does the teacher have to call Mommy?

My stay in Public School lasted less than 2 months.

"OK, Tovia, now you see what happens in Public School. They almost killed your son there!"

Mommy was exaggerating. There's only a little scar. "THANKS GOD YOU DIDN'T NEED NO STITCHES," she says.

7:30 AM—
We cross to Prospect Place.
MOMMY holds my hand
as we walk the 3 blocks
to my new school.

"Study good, Mattaleh," says
the ladies underwear and foundation man.

"You wouldn't have
to work so hard like me."

"You be a good student,
OK?" says the loafer.
"One day, maybe you will grow up
to be a WISE MAN, a *TALMUD CHOCHUM*.
Your *Mameh* would be proud."

"GOOD LUCK, MATTALEH,"
says the Pushcart Man— then,
"Listen, Gusta,
I got good new merchandise.

Maybe,
you'll take a look later?"

·Yeshiva— 1899 Prospect Avenue·

IZZY,
IKEY,
JAKEY,
SAM—
WE'RE
THE
BOYS
THAT
EAT
NO
HAM!

MOMMY

ME

1ST GRADE CHANUKAH PARTY

In the morning the Rabbi taught us how to be good Jews.

שְׁמַע
יִשְׂרָאֵל

We'd repeat the "Hear O Israel" prayer every day— eyes shut tight.

I learned my Hebrew letters

and began to read.

Recess was at 12—
An hour to play Box Baseball,
Chinese Handball, Hit the Penny, Tag,
Hide'n Seek, or Cowboys and Indians.

It was also lunchtime.

Mommy packed me
a meat sandwich—
EVERYDAY.
"You'll take,"
she says.
"You'll eat."

I HATED MEAT.
I didn't eat.

Instead, I threw
the sandwiches in the trash.

Not to worry, though— MATTALEH NEVER WENT HUNGRY.

I bought a potato knish from the **Knish Man.**

The taste of the fried onions and mashed potatoes was wonderful! I used his large metal saltshaker to add a TON of SALT. It was attached to a chain.

"One knish, please."

"So you little mamzers, bastards don't steal it," he says.

He arrived at lunchtime and stood just outside of the schoolyard.

That beat up metal cart he pushed kept the knishes piping hot.

"I do a good business by the **Yeshiva,**" he says. "My potato is the biggest seller. I also sell there 1-2 kasha knishes a day. Then, after lunchtime, I walked back to the PROSPECT PLACE MARKET to make more business."

Later in the year, a boy named Michael joined our class.

I was surprised when I heard his parents speak English without an accent.
They were AMERICAN-BORN— a novelty.

His Mom made 20 peanut butter and jelly sandwiches and froze them at the beginning of each month.
She defrosted one a day for Michael's lunch.

SOON WE STARTED TRADING SANDWICHES.
He loved the meat sandwiches.
I loved the peanut butter and jelly.

"Oy, Mattaleh, this is the first time I am hearing from these things.
How you can throw the lunch away or even give the lunch away— SUCH A SIN!
And also YOU paid the knishman for his knishes?
Every morning I paid this GONIFF 25 cents to give you a knish, too!

WHAT A THIEF!" MOMMY SAYS.

RECESS TIME was also a time for me and my friends Sol, Irving, Paul, and Joel to hatch PLOTS.

Heh, heh, heh.

Our 2nd grade English teacher alway sat at the top of the school steps when she was on recess patrol.

"Isn't she beautiful,"
I say.
"She's a knockout,"
Sol agrees.
"Think she
wears underwear?"
Irv asks, hopefully.

And so, to find out,
we organized a
"LOOK UNDER
THE TEACHER'S DRESS" game.

I bet she thought
we were playing the usual
Hide'n Seek or Tag...

After about 15 minutes
of running around with
our backs down,
and heads up—

RESULTS!

"She's wearing panties!" cries Joel. "I saw them!"
"What color? What color!" We all wanted to know.

"You gotta believe me.
They're pink, with
little flowers."

"Oy..."

I didn't ever get to see those panties but, until this day,
they remain etched in my memory...

We began the rest of our school day
by reciting
the PLEDGE of ALLEGIANCE—

It was "ENGLISH TIME."

I learned my letters.

And to read
and to write.

I learned to add.
I learned to subtract.

(Making change
for the customers
gave me a leg up
on my math.)

SCHOOL WAS OVER AT 5.
And I walked home.

MOMMY WAS NEVER HAPPY WITH ME.

"Look *Mameh*, I got a 98 on my spelling test," I say.

"*Nu*," she says. "Why not 100 percent?"

"Look Ma, I got an A
on my penmanship," I say.
"Why not an A+?" she says.

The grades Bernard and I brought home never seemed to satisfy Mommy.
SHE WANTED PERFECTION.

"No, Mattaleh, what you are thinking,
is not right," says *deh Mameh*.

"When I was a little girl, MY mother,
she should rest in peace,
didn't care what was my marks.
She don't let me study.
For her I only need to know to cook,
to sew, to keep a house.
And from MY father,
he should rest in peace, I hear
'A little girl don't need to be so smart.'

I ONLY WANTED FOR YOU AND BOYNAT
TO BE THE BEST."

242

I am absolutely convinced that at least some INQUISITION EXPERIENCE was key to employment at my Yeshiva.

Our first grade **Rabbi** kept a pint of sour milk on top of the book closet, for "THE BAD KIDS."

The fourth grade teacher kept a thumbscrew in his desk drawer— NO JOKE.

He used it quite a bit.

(At the time, I wanted to buy one and try it out on Bernard.)

If one of us was too loud
or we weren't paying attention,
Rabbi M.,
my 5th grade Hebrew teacher,
threatened to
"GET OUT THE WHIP."

Then he'd grab his belt,
wiggle it around,
and sing
at the TOP of his LUNGS.

"THIS BELT TASTES GOOD—
BOOM, BOOM—
LIKE A BELT SHOULD"—
This to the tune of the TV commercial,
"WINSTON TASTES GOOD—
BOOM, BOOM—
LIKE A CIGARETTE SHOULD."

Unlike the 4th grade teacher, Rabbi M. never hurt anyone.
For him the belt was more like the ATOM BOMB— strictly a deterrent.
He was really funny, this guy. I liked his class.
That year I mastered 10 pages of the TALMUD and recited them by heart—
first the Aramaic words and then the Yiddish translation.

My 7th grade English teacher, Mr. G., was never cruel—just hungry.
He was more interested in eating than teaching.

"Who wants to volunteer
to get me
some food?" he asks.

"Me!" "Me!" "Me!" "Me!" "Me!" "Me!" "Me!" "Me!" "Me!"

WE **ALL** WANTED TO BE
PICKED.
It was a way of
getting out of school,
<u>and</u>, Mr. G.
shared his eats.

The CHOSEN ONE
could always count
on a bite or a lick
of the snack—
on a good day he might
snag a whole YODEL!

"So Joel,
whaddya think?
You wanna get me
2 LEMON ICES,
some LEMON PIE,
or a couple of YODELS?
Here's some money.
Surprise me."

245

Joel went to Louie's, the candy store next to our school.

"2 lemon ices please, Mr. Louie."

Mr. Louie made his own lemon ices. It wasn't too sweet— tiny pieces of bitter lemon peel lay suspended in the ice.

IT WAS THE BEST ICES I'VE EVER TASTED.

"If I tell you my recipe, son, I'd have to kill you," he says.

"Great job," Mr. G. told Joel after he got back.

"YOU DID GOOD. Here, have a few licks."

That year Irv brought his HUGE HOARD of MAD magazines to school. We devoured them at recess.

MAD

MAD 25¢

THIS ISSUE WILL MAKE J.F.K.

MAD

I WANT YOU

He was lucky to have such a great collection. I SWEAR HE OWNED EVERY SINGLE ONE.

(Even though I was allowed to read the comics and magazines in Teddy's, I couldn't keep any.)

"Oy Mattaleh, another complaint from you... We had a business. You read, then you put back," Mommy says. "For sure, we needed to sell them.

Anyway, why you needed to keep this garbage? YOU ARE AN EDUCATED PERSON."

One day, Irv had a brainstorm. "Hey, who wants to help me make a funny news magazine?"

Paul and I signed on right away.

Irv proposed we call it ADMay. (Pig Latin was popular that year.)

Irv, of course, became the editor-in-chief.

After all, it was his idea.

"I'll write the news, but it'll be funny."

Paul picked Sports Editor— He was a whiz at baseball statistics.

"Ask me anything. Sandy Koufax's current ERA? I know it. Mickey Mantle's lifetime batting average? I know it."

"DIBS ON COMICS EDITOR," I insist.

I decided to draw an original comic hero that was a cross between my favorite magic lollipop licking superhero— HERBIE, the FAT FURY...

...and Mr. G.

Oh, I also stole a little from Superman.

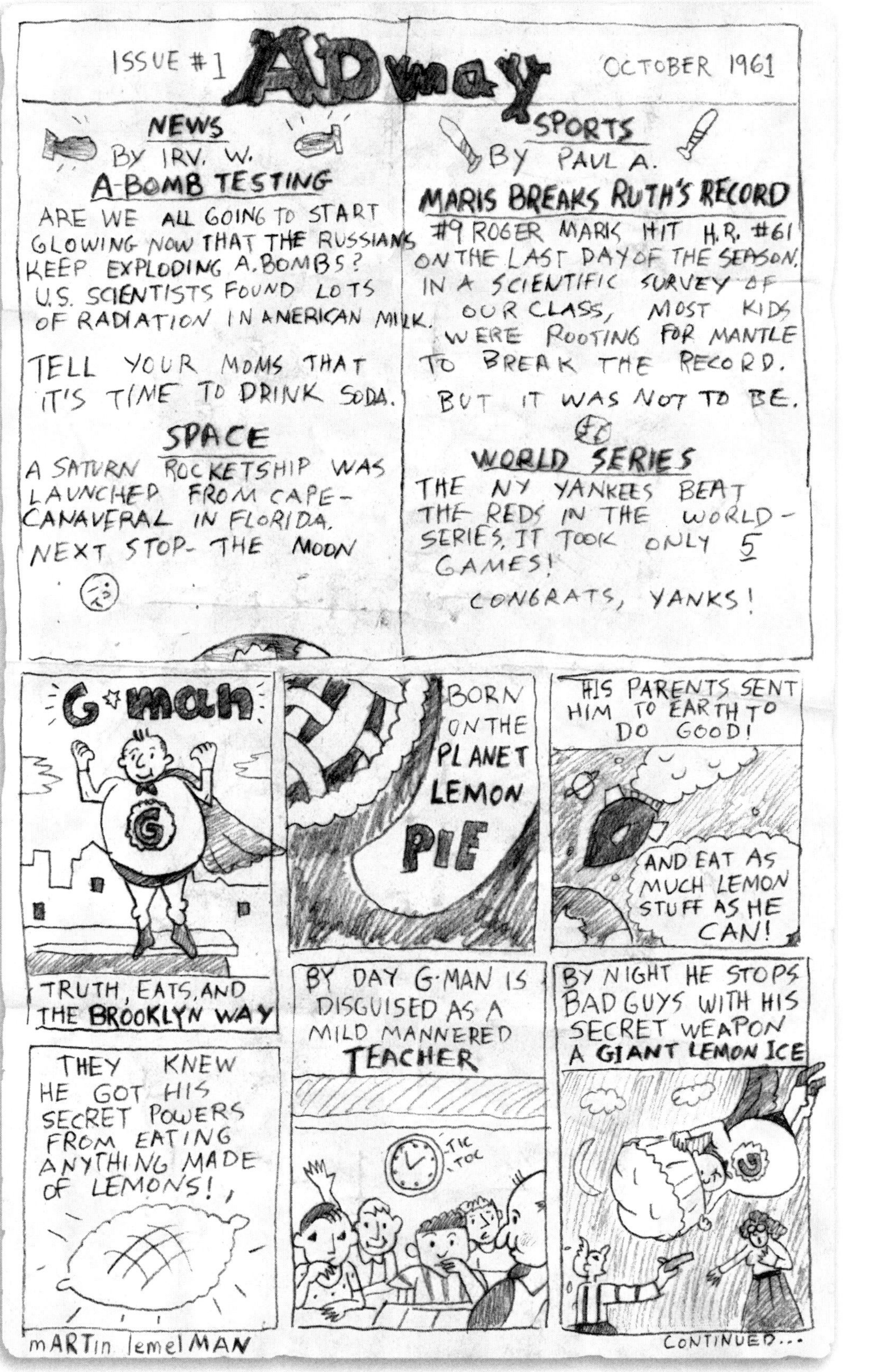
ISSUE #1
ADway
OCTOBER 1961
NEWS
BY IRV. W.
A-BOMB TESTING
ARE WE ALL GOING TO START GLOWING NOW THAT THE RUSSIANS KEEP EXPLODING A.BOMBS? U.S. SCIENTISTS FOUND LOTS OF RADIATION IN AMERICAN MILK.
TELL YOUR MOMS THAT IT'S TIME TO DRINK SODA.
SPACE
A SATURN ROCKETSHIP WAS LAUNCHED FROM CAPE-CANAVERAL IN FLORIDA.
NEXT STOP- THE MOON
SPORTS
BY PAUL A.
MARIS BREAKS RUTH'S RECORD
#9 ROGER MARIS HIT H.R. #61 ON THE LAST DAY OF THE SEASON. IN A SCIENTIFIC SURVEY OF OUR CLASS, MOST KIDS WERE ROOTING FOR MANTLE TO BREAK THE RECORD.
BUT IT WAS NOT TO BE.
WORLD SERIES
THE NY YANKEES BEAT THE REDS IN THE WORLD-SERIES, IT TOOK ONLY 5 GAMES!
CONGRATS, YANKS!
G-man
TRUTH, EATS, AND THE BROOKLYN WAY
BORN ON THE PLANET LEMON PIE
HIS PARENTS SENT HIM TO EARTH TO DO GOOD!
AND EAT AS MUCH LEMON STUFF AS HE CAN!
THEY KNEW HE GOT HIS SECRET POWERS FROM EATING ANYTHING MADE OF LEMONS!
BY DAY G-MAN IS DISGUISED AS A MILD MANNERED TEACHER
TIC TOC
BY NIGHT HE STOPS BAD GUYS WITH HIS SECRET WEAPON A GIANT LEMON ICE
mARTin lemelMAN
CONTINUED...

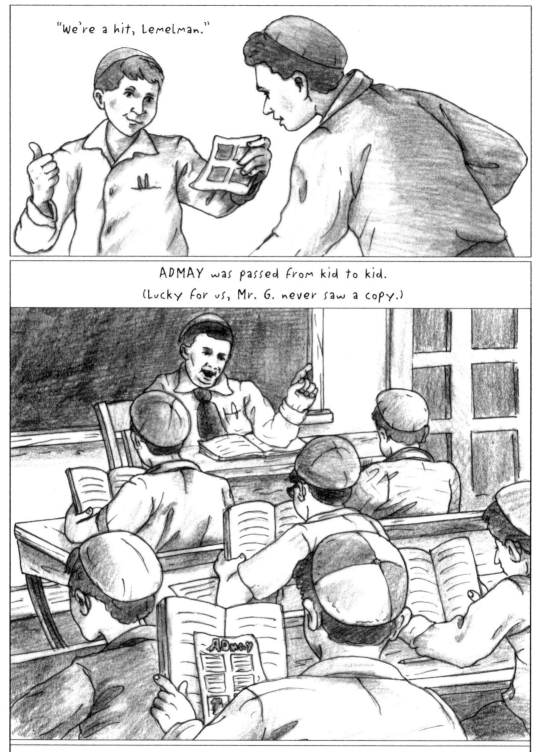

"We're a hit, Lemelman."

ADMAY was passed from kid to kid.
(Lucky for us, Mr. G. never saw a copy.)

The "staff" copied the 6 page magazine by hand— very tedious. Because of this, there were only a few copies an edition. So, after the fifth issue, we got tired of the whole business and went on to other things.

Most Saturdays, Irv, Sol, and I met at Paul's to play cards, checkers, or, when his parents weren't home, to make prank phone calls.

"Hello... YES?"

"Congratulations, MRS. GLICK! This is radio station, WMCA. AND... Believe it or not, you've won a FREE TRIP to Miami Beach!"

No one believed us, but it was fun anyway... WE WERE BAD.

One Saturday, I convince Sol to take the long walk up Eastern Parkway to the Brooklyn Museum. Paul and Irv don't want to come. "Why would we want to go to a museum?" they ask.

"To see what a real painting looks like," I answer.

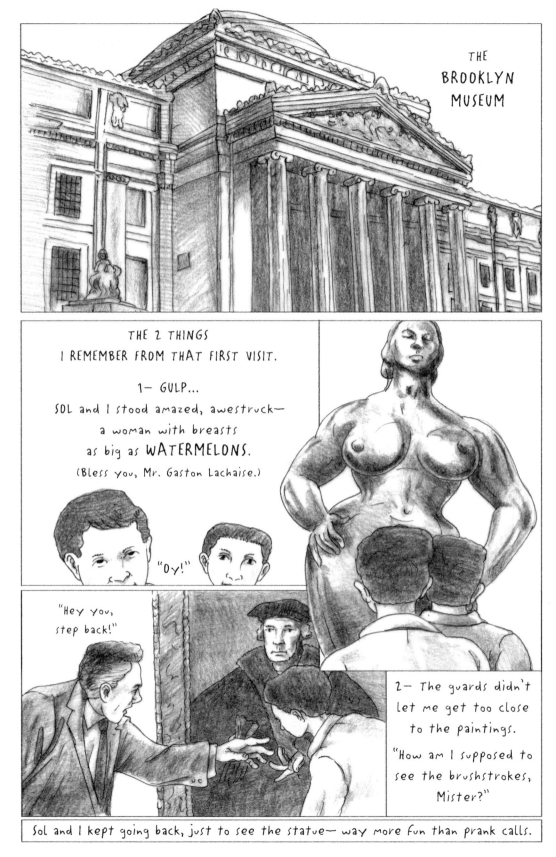

THE
BROOKLYN
MUSEUM

THE 2 THINGS
I REMEMBER FROM THAT FIRST VISIT.

1— GULP...
SOL and I stood amazed, awestruck—
a woman with breasts
as big as WATERMELONS.
(Bless you, Mr. Gaston Lachaise.)

"OY!"

"Hey you,
step back!"

2— The guards didn't
let me get too close
to the paintings.

"How am I supposed to
see the brushstrokes,
Mister?"

Sol and I kept going back, just to see the statue— way more fun than prank calls.

·1960·

Gott hut zich bashafen ah velt mit kleineh veltelach.
God created a world filled with little worlds.

Yiddish saying

·ALWAYS, TIME PASSES·

"You know, Mattaleh,
der tsayt went so fast.
In the blink of the eye,
you was a baby and now...

For me, was big changes, too.
It was like I opened the store
YESTERDAY.
But no, in 1960, I was 51 years."

The '50s crept into the '60s,
and our neighborhood was transformed.
You only had to glance at TEDDY'S newspaper stand to see how
BROWNSVILLE was different.
We were selling fewer Jewish Daily Forwards and
more of the La Prensa, El Diario
and the New York Amsterdam News.

"Now, I stick PORK RINDS on the same rack from the potato chips. **FEH!** But, this is business.

The COLORED PEOPLES and the SPANISH PEOPLES was asking for them.

"**This** stock was moving fast, very fast," says **Daddy**.

"We was ordering them every week."

"**NOW**, EGG CREAMS WE DIDN'T SELL SO MANY. But, the MINCK GRAPE SODA and PUNCH SODA— these made for us alotta money," says **Mommy**.

"You know what is funny? Peoples was also starting to buy more NO-CAL SODA.

"The AMERICANS are afraid to eat, to be FAT. They have a hope this NO-CAL will make them skinny.

Oy, they don't know what it is like to be hungry."

AFTER MIDNIGHT... I tossed and turned— couldn't sleep.
I slapped at the roach that I thought was crawling on me. But, it was just sweat.

I couldn't shut out the dogs barking, the faucets dripping, the cats hissing,
my parents snoring... It was so hot.

Even the breeze
through the window
didn't bring
any relief.

Instead, the breeze brought waves of SALSA MUSIC blasting from the radios and record players of our PUERTO RICAN neighbors. My bed vibrated.

Mommy and Daddy were so tired, a bomb wouldn't wake them.

The music seemed to soothe me and, after awhile, everything melted away. My eyelids shut. I fell asleep.

Exhausted.

Mommy, Bernard, and I rode the bus to the Eastern Parkway Arena to see J.F.K. — It's October 27th 1960, a day after my 10th birthday.

I was crushed by the crowd.

A NEW LEADER FOR THE 60's

KENNEDY FOR PRESIDENT

We waited for an hour until Robert F. Wagner introduced him.
"Who's Robert F. Wagner?" I ask Bernard.
"He's the Mayor, you idiot," my brother hisses. "Shhh, I'm listening."

The crowd went wild when Kennedy began to speak.
But, all I was thinking was, "How did he get such a dark tan? It's late in October."
It's funny, but that's all I remember about seeing our future president.

"**Mattaleh, Mattaleh**, you was a little boy from 10.
Why you should remember more?
What 10-year-old is interested in Politics?
BUT I, I REMEMBER EVERYTHING!

'I'm telling you Tovia, eight years
the Republicans was in the White House.
I figure, <u>now</u>, let the Democrats have a chance.
They deserve too. No?
MY VOTE IS FOR KENNEDY,'
this I told der Tateh.

I was surprised when he agreed with me."

...Ladies and gentlemen, I will make it brief, because
I know you have been standing for some time...

Let me give you five ways that MR. NIXON is frozen
in the ice of his own indifference.

No.1, we have the highest cost of living this week in
the history of the United States...

Secondly, because of the high interest rates of this
administration, if you buy a $10,000 home today on a
30-year mortgage, your interest rate on the loan is
$3,300 more than it was 8 years ago...

Three... this summer, 90 percent of the Republicans voted
against a minimum wage of $1.25 an hour...

*Four...*if you want to send your child to college today,
it costs you $1,300 more than it cost you in 1952.

Fifth, and finally, the question of which candidate
stands for opportunity to all Americans regardless of
their race, their creed or their color. In 1953 and 1954,
the Republican Party controlled the White House, the
Senate and the House, a majority of all bodies. Not one
civil rights bill was passed the light of day in either the
House or the Senate.

Everything that FRANKLIN ROOSEVELT and WOODROW WILSON
and HARRY TRUMAN tried to do, the Republican Party
stood against, and in 1960, in a great time of decision,
I come to BROOKLYN, and ask your help in picking this
country up and moving it forward again. THANK YOU.

On that day,
the kitchen
was the place to be.

The sweet scent of
bubbling vanilla syrup
blended with the perfume of
frying latkas.

This was the wooden bowl
where Mommy made
the potato pancake batter.

Deh Mameh always made the vanilla syrup
for the store.
She combined water, sugar, and vanilla extract
and boiled the mixture for hours.

It was cheaper than buying the ready-made kind.

OUR BIG VANILLA POT ⟶

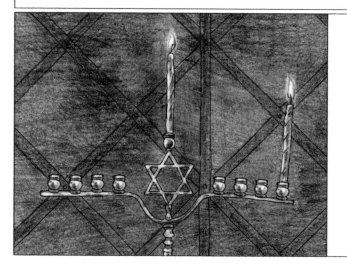

the first night of
CHANUKAH,
the festival of Lights,
<u>and</u>
VANILLA MAKING DAY.

AHHHH...
a good day.

"So, **Mameh**, how about
I have a little taste?
OK?
Nu, why not?

What if, maybe I help?
I can mix,
or I can fry for you.

Huh? I guarantee
you wouldn't be sorry.

I CAN MAKE THEM
REALLY *TASTY*.
You know I could.
It's no problem for me.
<u>PLEASE?</u>"

"GO OUT FROM HERE, MATTALEH!
You don't see I'm busy?
Go, play with Jan."

I couldn't
believe it.
Deh Mameh
NEVER
kicked me out
of the kitchen.

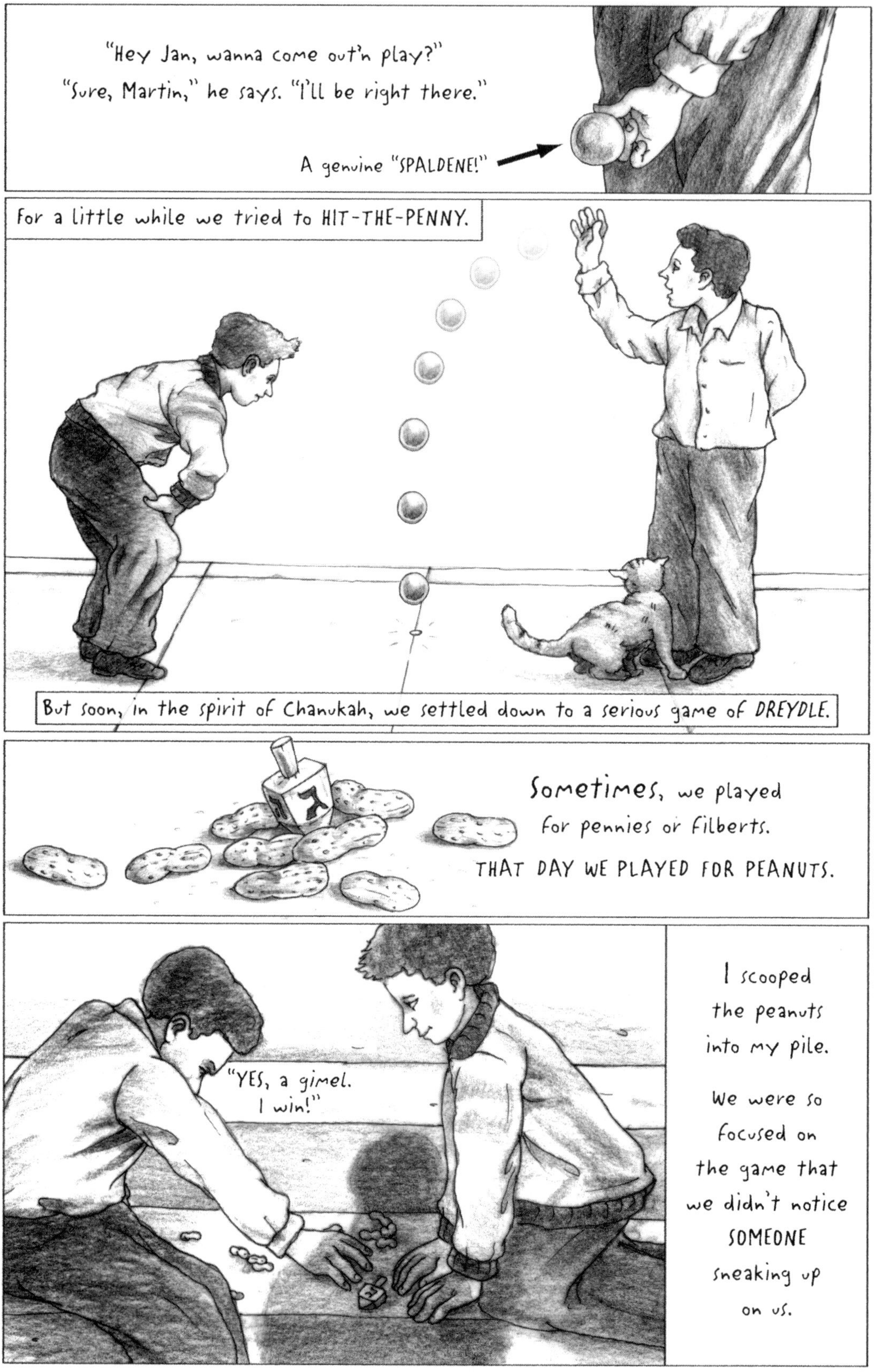
"Hey Jan, wanna come out'n play?"
"Sure, Martin," he says. "I'll be right there."
A genuine "SPALDENE!"
For a little while we tried to HIT-THE-PENNY.
But soon, in the spirit of Chanukah, we settled down to a serious game of DREYDLE.
Sometimes, we played for pennies or filberts.
THAT DAY WE PLAYED FOR PEANUTS.
"YES, a gimel. I win!"
I scooped the peanuts into my pile.
We were so focused on the game that we didn't notice SOMEONE sneaking up on us.

And then he's right there—
an older black kid,
holding a knife—
tiny but sharp.

"HEY, JEWBOYS,
GIMME
THEM
PEANUTS."

He cracked some into his mouth, stuffed the rest in his pockets, and raced away.

I COULDN'T BELIEVE HE ROBBED US— and for peanuts...
In those few moments, BROOKLYN changed for me.

The *Inky Boys.*

As he had often done before,
The woolly-headed black-a-moor
One sultry summer's day went out
To see the shops and walk about;

SUCH A BISINESS

Ainer vaist nisht dem anderens krenk.
One doesn't know the other's misfortune.

Yiddish saying

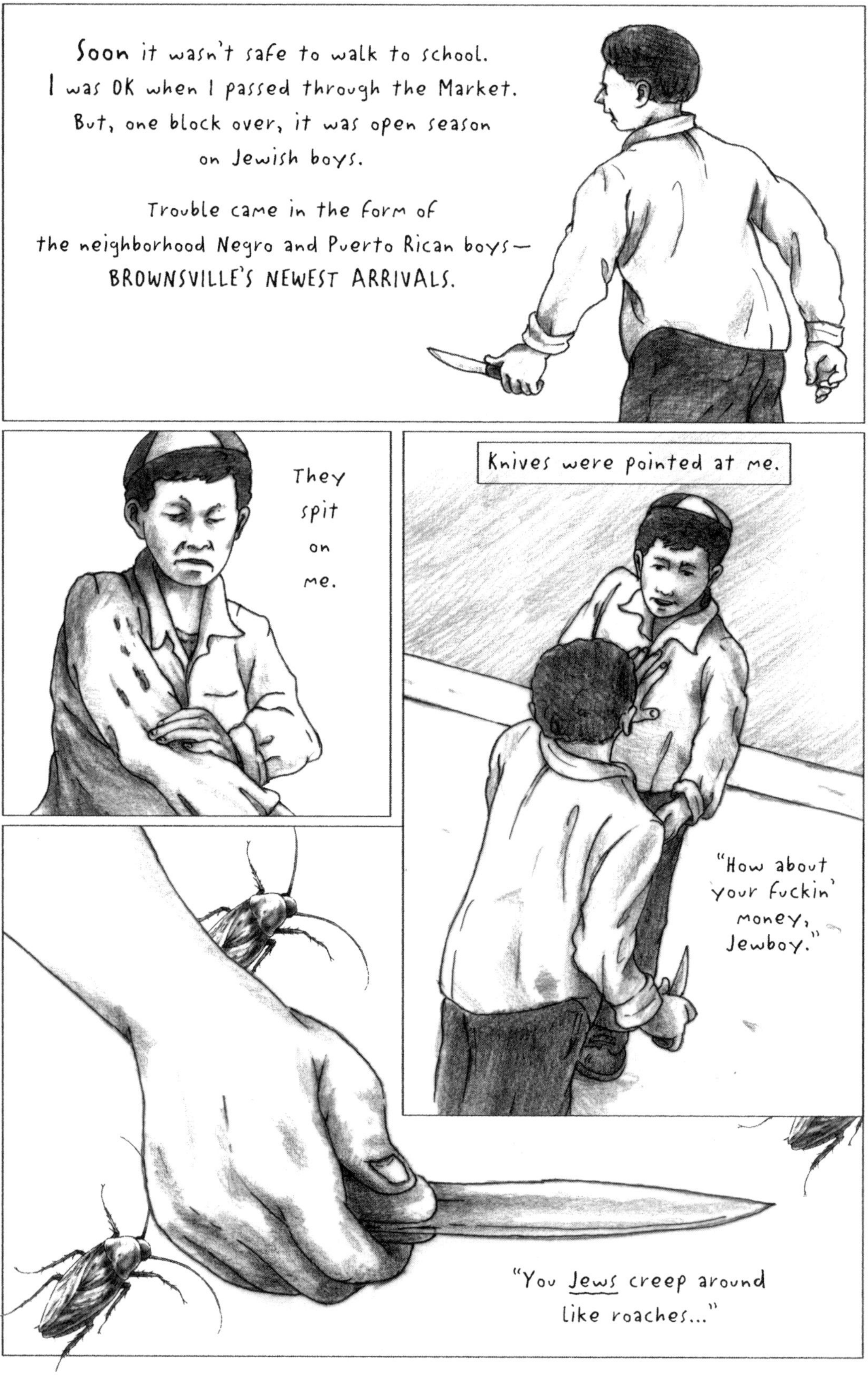
Soon it wasn't safe to walk to school. I was OK when I passed through the Market. But, one block over, it was open season on Jewish boys.
Trouble came in the form of the neighborhood Negro and Puerto Rican boys— BROWNSVILLE'S NEWEST ARRIVALS.
They spit on me.
Knives were pointed at me.
"How about your fuckin' money, Jewboy."
"You Jews creep around like roaches..."

I didn't know any of these boys.

But they ALL seemed to know me.

I was the boy with many names— "KIKE," "JEW BOY," "DIRTY JEW," "CHEAP JEW," "RICH JEW," "SMELLY JEW," "STUPID FUCK," "BEANIE BOY," and sometimes "THE JEW WHO KILLED JESUS."

"No, I did not kill JESUS," I protest.

"I wasn't born in JESUS'S time, and besides, JESUS was a Jew. Why would I want to kill him?"

"JESUS WASN'T NO JEW!" one of the boys snaps.
"YES, HE WAS," I insist, with authority.
"NO, HE WASN'T!" another one answers. "YES, HE WAS..."
Then, after a long pause, one of the cleverer ones wraps up the argument—
"EVEN IF JESUS WAS A JEW, HE CONVERTED ON THE CROSS. SO <u>THERE</u>, YOU LITTLE KIKE."

End of theological discussion. Time to get beaten up.

·SELF DEFENSE·

If there was one boy,
I'd punch and run.

If there were a bunch of kids,
I'd just run.

If he caught me, I'd fight.

I'd race as fast as the wind.

I never told Mommy.

"I knew, I knew," **deh Mameh** says.

"But what could I do? I'm seeing what is going on in the neighborhood and I'm thinking, maybe we should close the store? Who needs all this *tsuris*. My friend Etel is moving.

'GUSTA,' she told to me, 'THE AREA IS CHANGING. YOU WATCH AND SEE.'

"To be hated in BROWNSVILLE, for BROOKLYN to become another POLAND for us... the bitterness from this was almost too much for me.

"What was happening to you **Mattaleh**," says **deh Tateh**, "was happening all around the neighborhood.

DID _I_ KNOW WHAT TO DO? No."

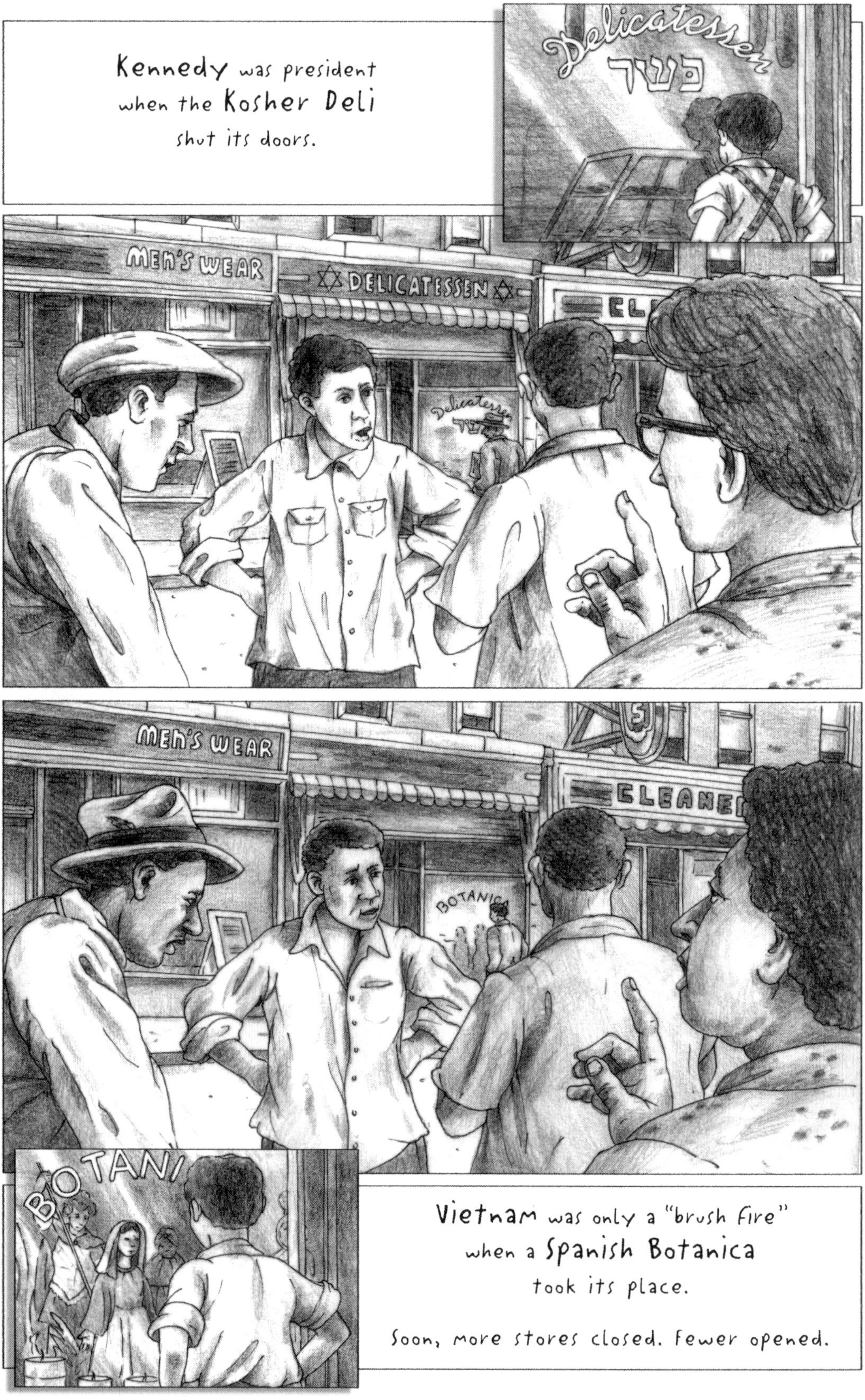
Kennedy was president when the Kosher Deli shut its doors.
Delicatessen
כשר
MEN'S WEAR
DELICATESSEN
Delicatessen
MEN'S WEAR
BOTANICA
Vietnam was only a "brush fire" when a Spanish Botanica took its place.
Soon, more stores closed. Fewer opened.

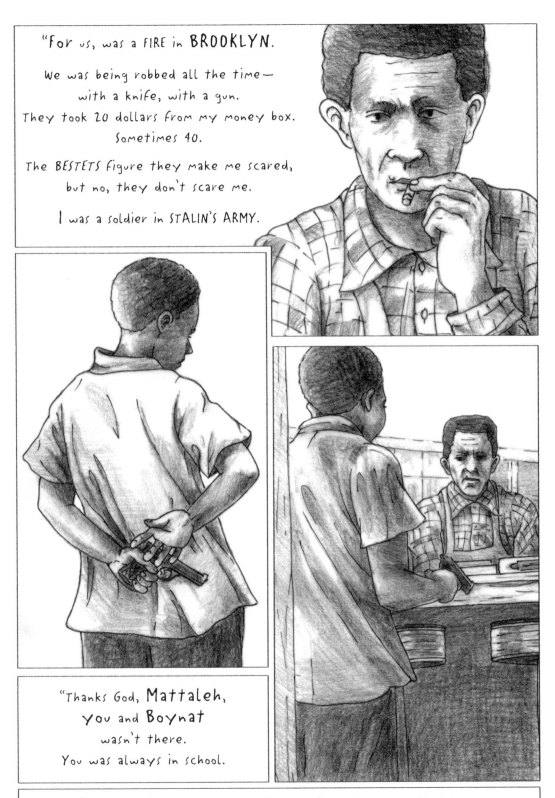

"For us, was a FIRE in BROOKLYN.

We was being robbed all the time—
    with a knife, with a gun.
They took 20 dollars from my money box.
    Sometimes 40.

The BESTETS figure they make me scared,
    but no, they don't scare me.

I was a soldier in STALIN'S ARMY.

"Thanks God, Mattaleh,
    you and Boynat
    wasn't there.
You was always in school.

"THE POLICE? They was good for nothing when we called them.
The neighborhood was in trouble, and THE POLICE was good for nothing."

Sounds of wailing greeted me when I came home from school one day. I can't forget the ribbons of spit, the row of black stitches that lined MOMMY's gums.

What a terrible day— the dentist pulled her top teeth in the morning, and a robber pulled a gun in the afternoon.

AIEEEE, AIEEEE, ... EE, AIEE
AIEEEE, AIE ... EE, AIEE
AIEEEE, A ... EE, AIEE
AIEEEE, ... EE, AIEE
AIEEE ... AIEE
AIE ... AIEE
AIEEEE, ... AIEE
AIEEEE, ... EEE, AIEE
AIE ... EE

"...Negro male, about 20 years old— that right, Teddy?"

"Yes, like this."

THEY NEVER CAUGHT ANYBODY.

"**We're** anti-exploitation and in this country THE JEWS have been located in the so-called NEGRO COMMUNITY as merchants and businessmen for so long that they feel guilty when you mention that the exploiters of NEGROES are JEWS. This doesn't mean that we are anti-Jews or anti-Semitic— WE'RE ANTI-EXPLOITATION."

MALCOLM X

"**This** gentleman makes me laugh. Don't he know THE JEWS come into BROWNSVILLE <u>first</u>?

WE MADE THE COMMUNITY NICE. Yes, was always some COLORED PEOPLES in our neighborhood, but most of the svartzes came in the 1960s. THEY LIVED IN <u>OUR</u> NEIGHBORHOOD, IN <u>OUR</u> BROOKLYN!

"**This** also makes me so mad when I hear how we was cheating them, how we was charging them too much. **Tell** me, in what store could you get a 5 cent soda or a 5 cent ice cream? This 5 cents was until 1968— nowhere you could get this but **Teddy's Candy Store.**

Your father made us a living in the store, but he didn't cheat NOBODY. WE WAS POOR WHEN WE STARTED THE STORE.

AND WE ENDED POOR."

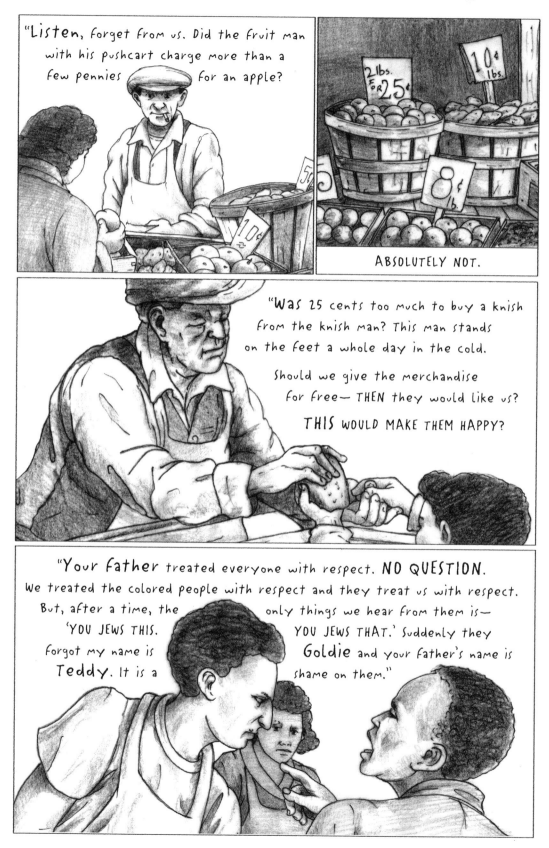

"Listen, forget from us. Did the fruit man with his pushcart charge more than a few pennies for an apple?

ABSOLUTELY NOT.

"Was 25 cents too much to buy a knish from the knish man? This man stands on the feet a whole day in the cold.

Should we give the merchandise for free— THEN they would like us?

THIS WOULD MAKE THEM HAPPY?

"Your father treated everyone with respect. NO QUESTION. We treated the colored people with respect and they treat us with respect. But, after a time, the only things we hear from them is— 'YOU JEWS THIS. YOU JEWS THAT.' Suddenly they forgot my name is Goldie and your father's name is Teddy. It is a shame on them."

"**Stacy** still came in for his cigarettes, but he was like a different person."

"What, Stacy, you forgot the Yiddish?" the father says.

"That ain't no language of mine," he answers.

"In late 1961, I had enough. I put the foot down to **der Tateh**," says Mommy.

"OK, we would keep the store, but we was moving from the back—

NO QUESTION!

"Your father was so angry from this decision. But... I don't care. I wanted a nice life for the children."

Safe and harmless

COMMENDED BY PARENTS

COOKIE

TABLETS

JACK FROST
CANE SUGAR

Tide
THE WASHDAY

SALT   PEPPER

Ehr kert iber di velt.
He turns the world upside down.

Yiddish saying

WE MOVED ON A TUESDAY.

MOMMY hired the WISE potato chip deliveryman to truck our stuff to 512 Saratoga Avenue.

"You take me, I pay you good."

WE filled cardboard boxes with clothing, dishes, photographs, and my grandmother's needlework. There wasn't much.

The only furniture we loaded was our free TV.

Thank goodness, we didn't take everything. The apartment, was on the 5th floor— and no elevator.

512

We all helped lug the stuff up the stairs— that is, except for **deh Tateh**.

He didn't want anything to do with "THIS NONSENSE."

"feh, this is a crazy idea."

Deh Mameh caught shopping fever. She bought new bedroom sets, a kitchen table and chairs, a sofa (covered in plastic, very fancy), a...

EVERYTHING WE NEEDED FOR OUR APARTMENT.

"I'm expecting a good deal, Mister!"

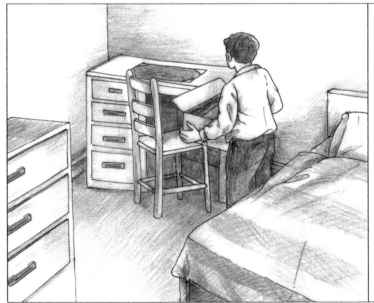

"Why you waste all the money?" says **Daddy**. "We have good furniture in the store."

"What else should we do with the money, **Tovia**?" **Mommy** answers. "Do you want to save it for the grave?"

I LOVED THIS NEW PLACE.

WHAT WASN'T TO LOVE?

Bernard and I had our own rooms— no more snoring parents or noisy refrigerators.

"Look, Ma, I can see Pitkin Avenue from the living room window."

"You like, no?" MOMMY says. "Vere iz shayne, ich been klig. Some are pretty, but I'm smart. I can sit in front from a mirror and put on lipstick, like a normal person."

Soon after we settled in, the toilet overflowed.

That's how I first met the janitor, Mr. Super. "I'll get you shittin' in no time, kiddo," he says to me.

He was right.

Bernard and I still went to the store after school— to help out, to do our homework and read comics.

We headed home around 7 or 8.

Sometimes Mommy would come with us.

Mostly, Bernard and I set off alone— a fifteen-minute walk.

Actually, we ran more than walked.

It was open season on Kikes.

Mommy and Daddy got home later.

When we got back, we'd take our shoes off, grab a bite and begin our matches.

THE LIVING ROOM WAS OUR RING.

Sad to say, even with all of my careful study of TV wrestling, Bernard usually slammed me to the floor and won.

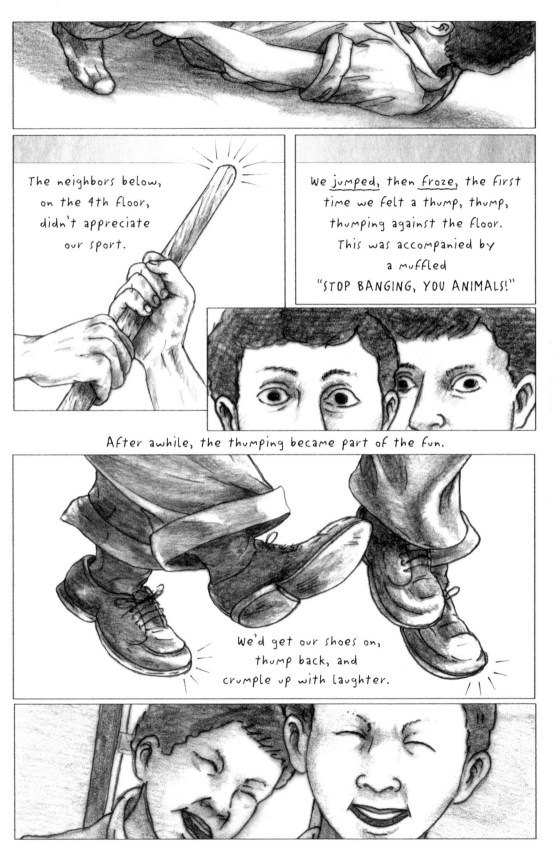

The neighbors below, on the 4th floor, didn't appreciate our sport.

We jumped, then froze, the first time we felt a thump, thump, thumping against the floor. This was accompanied by a muffled "STOP BANGING, YOU ANIMALS!"

After awhile, the thumping became part of the fun.

We'd get our shoes on, thump back, and crumple up with laughter.

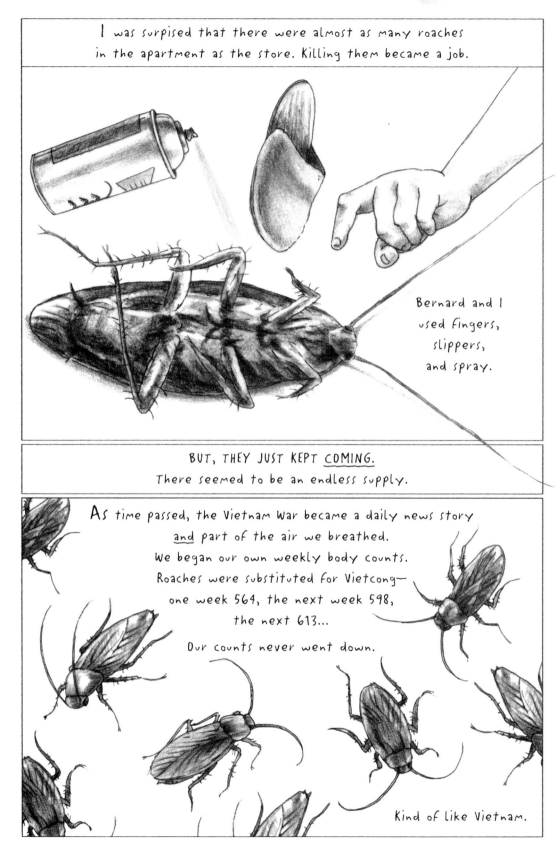

I was surpised that there were almost as many roaches in the apartment as the store. Killing them became a job.

Bernard and I used fingers, slippers, and spray.

BUT, THEY JUST KEPT COMING.
There seemed to be an endless supply.

As time passed, the Vietnam War became a daily news story and part of the air we breathed.
We began our own weekly body counts.
Roaches were substituted for Vietcong—
one week 564, the next week 598,
the next 613...

Our counts never went down.

Kind of like Vietnam.

·PITKIN AVENUE·

"Mattaleh, you want to go shpatzirin with me?" Mommy asks. "Come, we'll go for a walk on the Avenue."

Deh Mameh was as eager to explore the new neighborhood as I was.

The stores went on for blocks.

For every one in the PROSPECT PLACE MARKET, there were 10 on PITKIN AVENUE.

We walked past the LOEW'S PITKIN, an ARTHUR MURRAY DANCE STUDIO ("How can such a place make business?" Mommy wonders), SHOE STORES, CLOTHING STORES, a DELI, a HOLE IN THE WALL selling schmaltz herring and pumpernickel bread, a CAFETERIA, a CHINESE RESTAURANT ("Feh, who would want to eat this food?" Mommy says.)

A Pizza Parlor stopped Mommy in her tracks.

"How about we buy some slices pizza pie?" she asks me.

"It's not kosher, Mameh," I answer.

"Oy, don't you worry. I'll take THE SIN on me."

"Tam Gan Eden!"

And, that's how the deal was done. Mommy and I enjoyed our first pizza pie— a slice and a Coke for 25 cents. (The sin was on her.)

A few weeks later, the magic of PITKIN AVENUE faded for me.

One night, while walking home, I spied a huge rat crawling through hot dogs, specials, and knishes— exploring the front window of the DELI.

·FUNERAL·

Nobody I knew died when we lived at 512 Saratoga Avenue. Yet, I attended a "funeral" almost every week— with **Daddy** as Master-of-Ceremonies...

It's late. I think **Mommy** and **Bernard** are asleep.

BRIGHT FLUORESCENT TUBES
LIGHT UP THE ROOM.

Daddy's in the kitchen—
chain-smoking, drinking, talking to himself.

"You want a GODDAMN partner? NO! We could have been MILLIONAIRES— collecting rents, not paying. We could have owned apartment buildings. We could have owned a farm. But, NO. She don't listen. SHE don't help. The LADY and her lousy family. We could be living in YOUNGSVILLE, today— We could live in a place with cows, NOT cockroaches!"

levaya, I'll give you a funeral. I came to this COUNTRY without a partner. Now, do I have a Here I am working like an animal, paying lousy rent. We could paying. We

The light bled
into my room.

"I need to sleep,"
I muttered
to myself.
I was trembling,
exhausted,
furious.

TOMORROW WAS A
SCHOOL DAY.

"WHY DON'T YOU
JUST SHUT UP!"
I wanted to yell.

Instead,
I got up...

...and shut
the kitchen light.

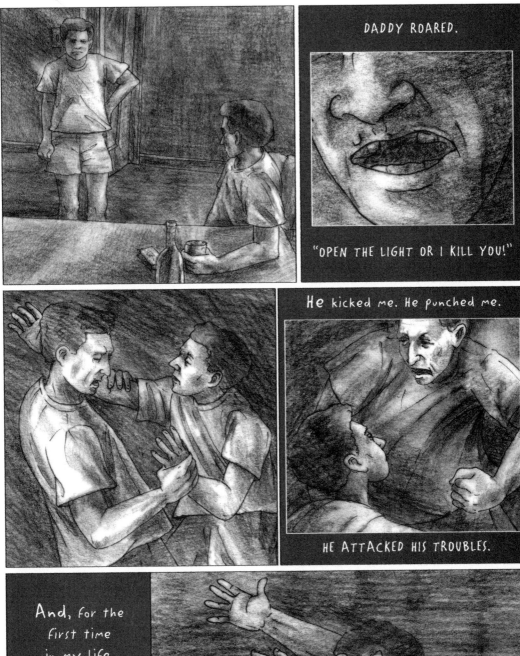

DADDY ROARED.

"OPEN THE LIGHT OR I KILL YOU!"

He kicked me. He punched me.

HE ATTACKED HIS TROUBLES.

And, for the first time in my life, I hit back.

I swear, that night, I was as crazy as DEH TATEH.

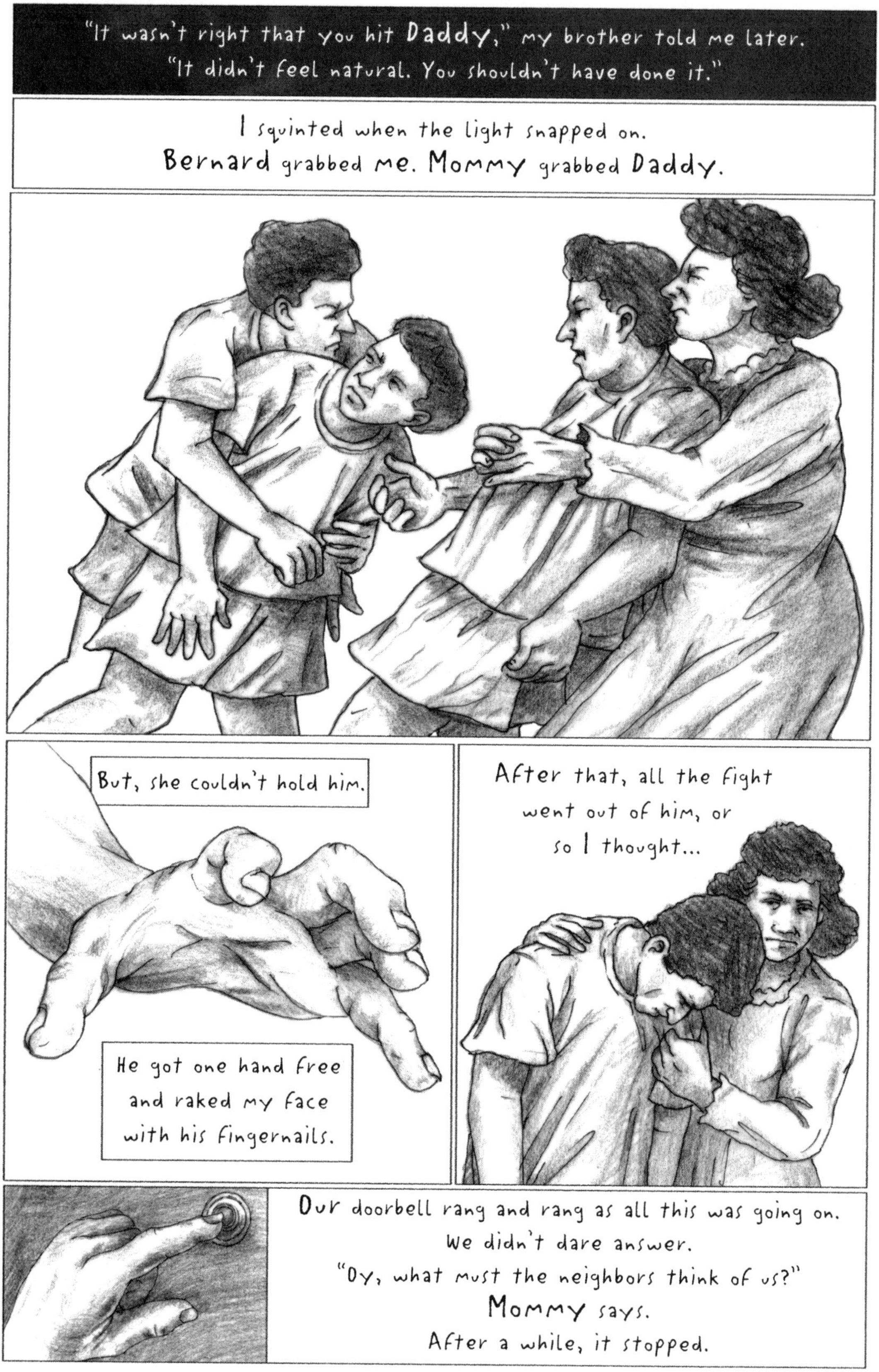
"It wasn't right that you hit Daddy," my brother told me later.
"It didn't feel natural. You shouldn't have done it."
I squinted when the light snapped on.
Bernard grabbed me. Mommy grabbed Daddy.
But, she couldn't hold him.
He got one hand free and raked my face with his fingernails.
After that, all the fight went out of him, or so I thought...
Our doorbell rang and rang as all this was going on.
We didn't dare answer.
"Oy, what must the neighbors think of us?"
Mommy says.
After a while, it stopped.

As I drifted off to sleep,
I heard cloth tearing.

Daddy went into the closet
and ripped
my Bar Mitzvah suit
apart.

"Don't you worry, Mattaleh,"
Mommy assured me.
"I promise. I will fix."

The next day,
she came home early and
sewed my suit back up.

"You see, Mattaleh,"
she said,
"is good like new.
I MAKE PROIFECT!"

And she did.

·THE SHUL AT 425 HOWARD·

It was Tuesday,
October 15, 1963—
The fall holidays were over.
My Bar Mitzvah
was only weeks away.

I hurried to keep
my first appointment
with the Rabbi of our Synagogue.

"So Mordechai," he asks me,
"are you prepared to recite
your Haftorah portion?"

BOY, WAS I PREPARED.

After 4 months of studying,
I practically knew the portion by heart.

Without a doubt, my beautiful chanting
was going to knock
the Rabbi dead.

"Lamah somar
Yaakov ootehda..."

OY YOY YOY, THE MEETING DIDN'T GO AS PLANNED...

Almost immediately,
the Rabbi raises his hand.

"Stop. STOP! Mordechai,"
he says. "This is not right.
Tell me, why do you layne
the LECH LECHA Haftorah,
when your birthday falls
on the VAYERAH portion,
a week after?"

I had a little over two weeks
to learn to sing
another Haftorah.

"Aieee," I thought, miserably, "I'VE BEEN STUDYING THE WRONG CHAPTER. With my luck, I should have known this would happen."

4 MONTHS EARLIER...

"Mattaleh, I got you an A-1 teacher for the 'Bal' Mitzvah lessons," deh Mameh said. "You gonna learn so good from him. He is so educated!"

And so began my Bar Mitzvah lessons.

For an hour, 2 times a week, the A-1 teacher and I sat in back of the store, preparing for the day that I would become A MAN.

He taught me to recite my portion. (Unfortunately, the incorrect one.) I also learned to decipher trop, ancient Hebrew musical notations— the key to every Haftorah portion.

"Mapach, pashta, zakayeyeyef, katon."

"Very good, Mordechai," he'd say, as he crammed a pinch of snuff into a nostril. He'd sneeze, then honk into his filthy handkerchief.

This procedure was repeated throughout the lesson.

BAR MITZVAH
Saturday, November 2, 1963

"V'eeshah achas minshay
b'nai haneveeyim
tsawakaw el Elisha laymor
avdehcha eeshee mayss..."

My recitation of
the new HAFTORAH
wasn't great,
but at least
I didn't embarrass
deh Mameh and
deh Tateh.

Bernard, Mommy, Daddy, and the shul regulars celebrated after
the service. "Much success, Muttle. You should have Mazel your whole life."
We all shared herring, pumpernickel, sponge cake, and honey cake.
I even drank a little schnapps. IT BURNED!

No relatives
or friends
were invited.

A little over 3 weeks later I attended my first real levaya.
In fact, the whole country did.
We all visited Dallas with President Kennedy.
We all watched as his casket moved through the streets of Washington, D.C.,
to the cemetery at Arlington.

It was just after my Bar Mitzvah that I decided to become an artist.

"Mattaleh, you would have been such a good doctor," says Mommy. "This I know for sure."

THE YEARS RUSHED BY.
I drew. I studied. I studied. I painted.
Most of our high school senior class was either going to BROOKLYN COLLEGE (if you had "the average") or HUNTER COLLEGE (if you didn't).

"C'mon Lemelman, you can't be serious."

A friend put his arm around me, (as if to comfort a crazy person), when I told him I was going to major in art.

In June 1967, I gave the Valedictorian speech. In September 1967, I'd begin BROOKLYN COLLEGE.

I couldn't wait for my first art class...

· ENOUGH ·

Az Got vut gelebt oif di velt, volt min alleh fenster oisgeshlogen.
If God lived on earth, we'd break all his windows.

Yiddish saying

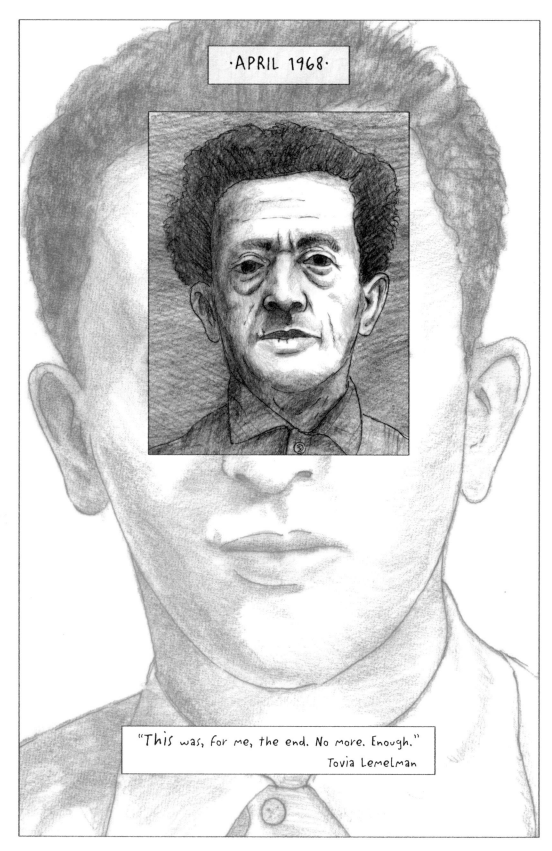

·APRIL 1968·

"This was, for me, the end. No more. Enough."
Tovia Lemelman

ONE BY ONE THE JEWS DISAPPEARED FROM BROWNSVILLE—
the one with the vest, the one with the dirty apron,
the ones with pockets bulging with change, the ones with no money,
the one who held a cigar he never smoked,
the one who built miniature wooden synagogues for a hobby,
the skinny ones, the fat ones,
the grey beards,
the yentas, the schnorers, the shleppers,
the meshugener,
the shlimazel...

PEOPLE I DIDN'T KNOW, DIDN'T RECOGNIZE, FILLED THE STREETS.
They were different.
They spoke Spanish or English with a thick Southern accent.

The
Prospect Place
Market
first shrunk,
then shriveled.

In 1968,
it disappeared
altogether.

Teddy's was one of the few
Jewish stores that still dotted
the neighborhood.
It remained essentially the same—
Daddy still got up every morning
to do the papers.
Mommy did the bills.

But, deh Tateh's LANDSLEIT
were all gone...

They departed for East Flatbush, Flatbush, Canarsie, Boro Park, Brighton Beach, and Sheepshead Bay... I heard some even went as far as the Bronx.

Blacks and Puerto Ricans
had taken their place.

This made no difference
to my father.

"AH CUSTOMER IS AH CUSTOMER,"
he says. "EVERYONE USES
THE SAME COLOR MONEY."

"One minute you believe your life will always be the same, The next minute your life changes forever. MY WHOLE LIFE I KNOWED THIS.

The end came a week after they kill Martin Luther King. We heard from riots, fires... This was for us, a dangerous time.

"The Last Day was slow.

We couldn't figure out.

No one, but no one, was coming into the store.

"We wasn't even making one penny.

"Ah, but after a time, a customer.

FINALLY, a customer..."

"A young black man comes in— quiet, not even a hello.

His mouth was closed, serious.

"I turned away from him. I am thinking, 'LET HIM LOOK.'

"Then, so quick, so quick, he comes in back of me.

"A knife was in his hand."

"HE GRABBED ME BY THE NECK,
and pardon me for the language,
he screams to your father,
'Gimme all your fuckin' money,
you dirty Jew,
or I'll cut this bitch's throat!'

Mattaleh,
what happened next
you wouldn't believe."

"Leave deh lady alone," your father says.

"I got deh money
HERE.
Take it and you go, OK?
PLEASE.

We don't want
no trouble."

"Der Tateh, the father spoke so calm. I never seen him so calm.

"He picked up
the money box to show."

"What happens next, you ask?" Daddy says.

"I throwed the damn box in the *bestet's punim.*

"WITH ALL MY KOACH, I THROWED IT GOOD.

"Money was flying this way and that way. The *sahnahvabitch* was bleeding from all over the face."

"He let go of **der Mameh,** and ran so fast away."

"**You** should never forget this, **Mattaleh,**" **Mommy** says, "that even with ALL our fighting, with ALL the anger and the bad words, <u>STILL</u> YOUR FATHER LOVED ME.

"He saved my life."

"In Poland, I ran away from the Nazis.
LIKE A DOG, I RAN FROM MY FATHER'S HOUSE.

"And now...
to be chased from YOUR FATHER'S STORE— IN AMERICA.
TO TREMBLE— IN AMERICA.

How could this be? How much can one person take?

"We went.

"Never again did I see TEDDY'S CANDY STORE."

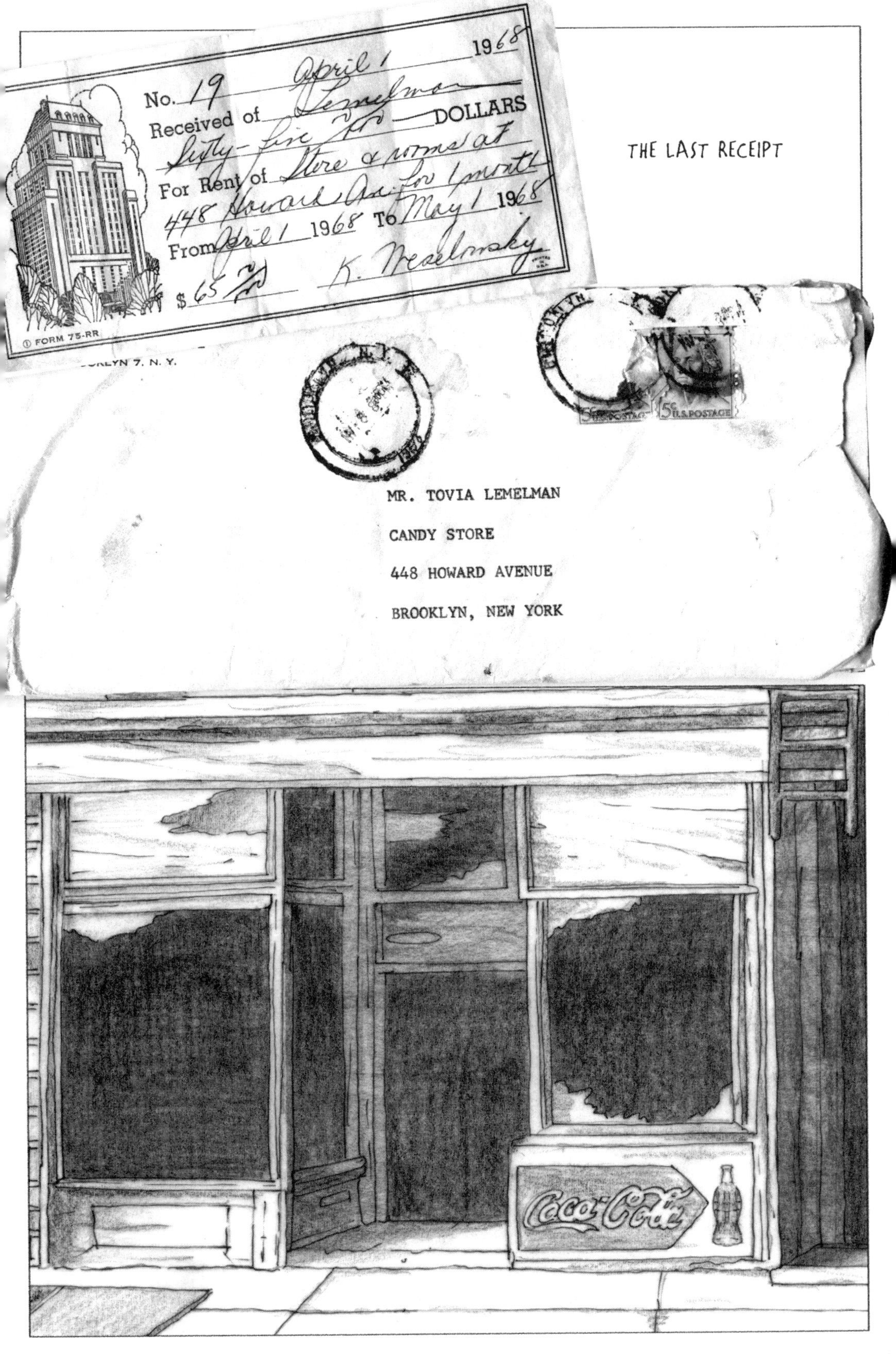
THE LAST RECEIPT
No. 19
April 1 1968
Received of Lemelman
Sixty-five DOLLARS
For Rent of Store & rooms at
448 Howard Av. for 1 month
From April 1 1968 To May 1 1968
$ 65
FORM 75-RR
5¢ U.S. POSTAGE
MR. TOVIA LEMELMAN
CANDY STORE
448 HOWARD AVENUE
BROOKLYN, NEW YORK
Coca-Cola

Di tseit ken allis ubermachen.
Time can change everything.

Yiddish saying

In the 1970s Mommy and Daddy moved to Far Rockaway, New York.

"*Deh Tateh* made such a beautiful garden in the back from our house. It was such a pleasure to walk to the beach together," says Mommy. "THIS WAS THE LIFE FOR ME.

In 1977 we became GRANDPARENTS for the first time.

Jonathan

1978

FINALLY, I THINK, YOUR FATHER WAS HAPPY.

I took good care from him when he became sick with the lung cancer and, in December 30, 1984, he passed away.

He should rest in peace.

1992

"Then, the time ran on...

In my final years, I was so happy to make VERENIKAS for my beloved grandchildren.

They ate them up and begged for more."

On December 8, 1996, Bernard phoned me from Mommy's house. "Martin," he said, "now, we're orphans."

I went to see deh Mameh for the last time.

It's been 25 years since Daddy passed away—
13 years since Mommy passed away.

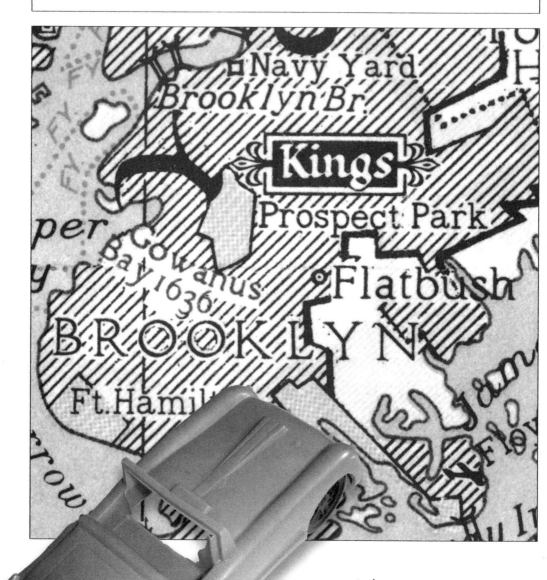

I drove the Prius back to Brooklyn
to see what was left of my childhood.

Next month, I'll be 59 years old.

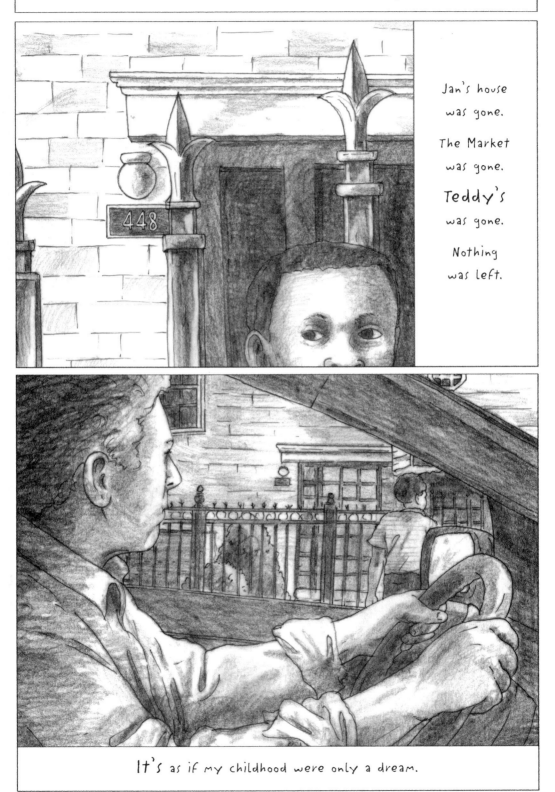

Jan's house was gone.

The Market was gone.

Teddy's was gone.

Nothing was left.

It's as if my childhood were only a dream.

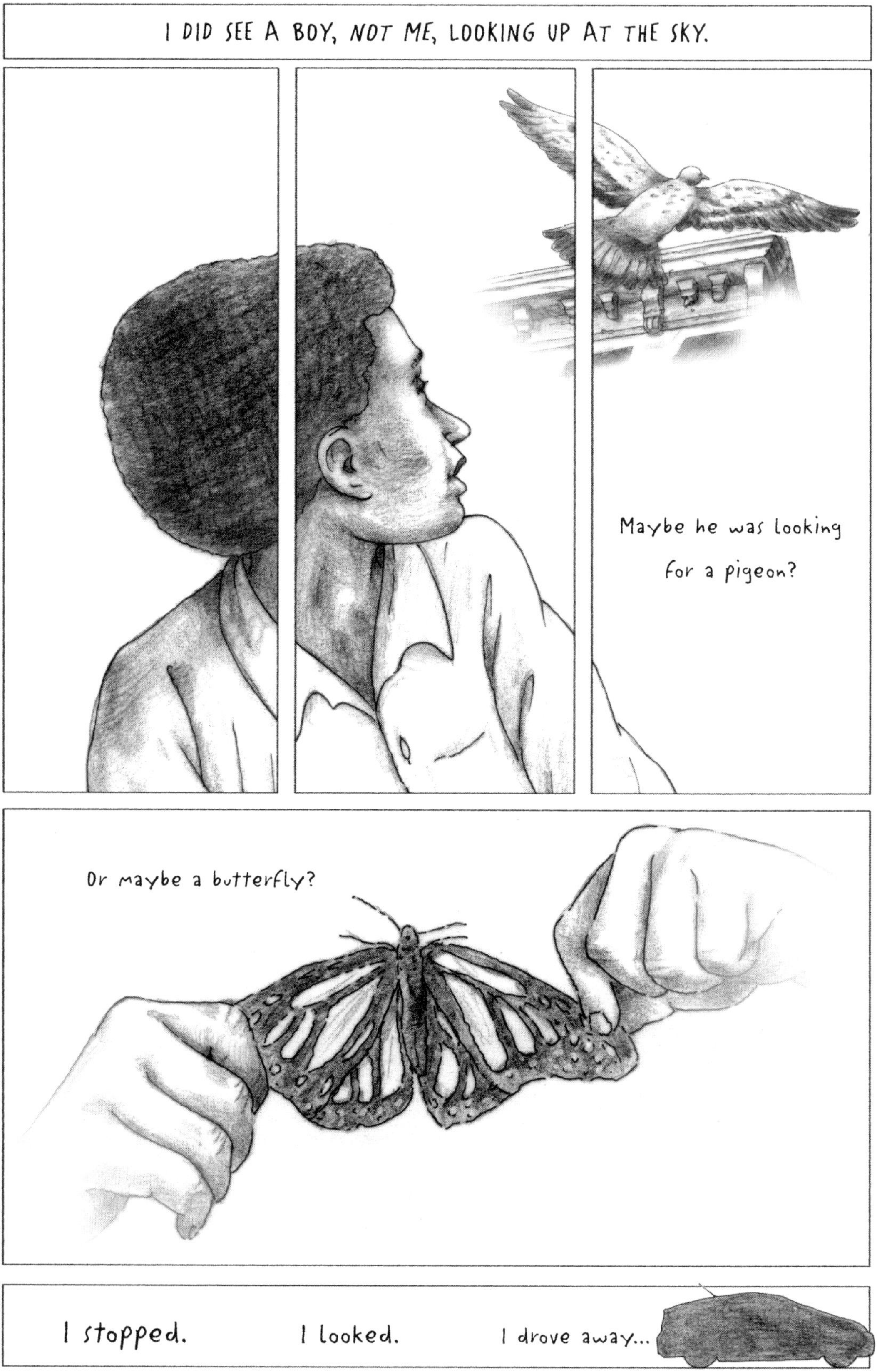
I DID SEE A BOY, *NOT ME*, LOOKING UP AT THE SKY.
Maybe he was looking for a pigeon?
Or maybe a butterfly?
I stopped.
I looked.
I drove away...

·ACKNOWLEDGMENTS·

Thank you, Mameh and Tateh, for giving me an interesting childhood.

Thank you, Tateh, for your years of hard work in a new country and trying your best for our family.

Thank you, Mameh, for saving report cards, bills, photographs, receipts, envelopes, certificates, EVERYTHING— you helped me touch my memories.

I'm grateful to my brother, Bernard, and to my agent, Rob McQuilkin, for their support. Their almost identical advice, about a year into this project, helped make this a better book.

Thanks to Kathy Belden, my editor at Bloomsbury Publishing, for her faith in the book and convincing me to create a TWO CENTS PLAIN version 2.0.

Thank you, Uncle Isia, Isak Schachter, for your insights.

Thank you, Shari Spark, Coordinator of the Lehigh Valley Holocaust Resource Center, for supplying me with original source material on Displaced Persons Camps.

I appreciate the many years of support and best wishes from my colleagues at Kutztown University. Thank you, Professors David Bullock, Nunzio Alagia, John Landis, Dennis Johnson, Tom Quirk, Kevin McCloskey, Laurel Bonhage, Todd Mcfeely, Kate Clair, Elaine Cunfer, Miles DeCoster, Brenda Innocenti, Karen Kresge, Dean Ballas, Vicki Meloney, and Denise Bosler, as well as Kathy Sue Traylor and Lucy Williams.

I'm also thankful to the many, many delightful and energetic Communication Design students I've had the privilege of teaching. Their abundant enthusiasm rubbed off on me.

Thank you Morris Dorsky, former chairperson of the Brooklyn College Art Department. You had faith in me— when I needed it. Rest in peace.

I'm proud and amazed to be the father of four great kids. Thank you, Jonathan, for your encouragement and for transcribing hours of interviews. Thank you, David, for your good humor and allowing me use of the "reference" in your house. Walking across the Brookyn Bridge with Allison was helpful. Thank you, Benjamin, for your always valuable counsel, your photography, and for being the "punctuation policeman." Thank you, Sam, for not letting me forget what a 16-year-old is like and for your naive drawing style.

Above all, thanks go to my dear wife, Monica. Although I growl at you when you suggest changes, you're usually right. I love you.

·ICE CREAM FOR EVERYBODY·

A Note on the Author

Martin Lemelman is the author
and illustrator of *Mendel's Daughter*
and has illustrated over thirty books
for children. His work has been published
in magazines ranging from the *New York
Times Book Review* to *Sesame Street* magazine.
He lives in Allentown, Pennsylvania, with
his wife, Monica. They are the
proud parents of four sons.

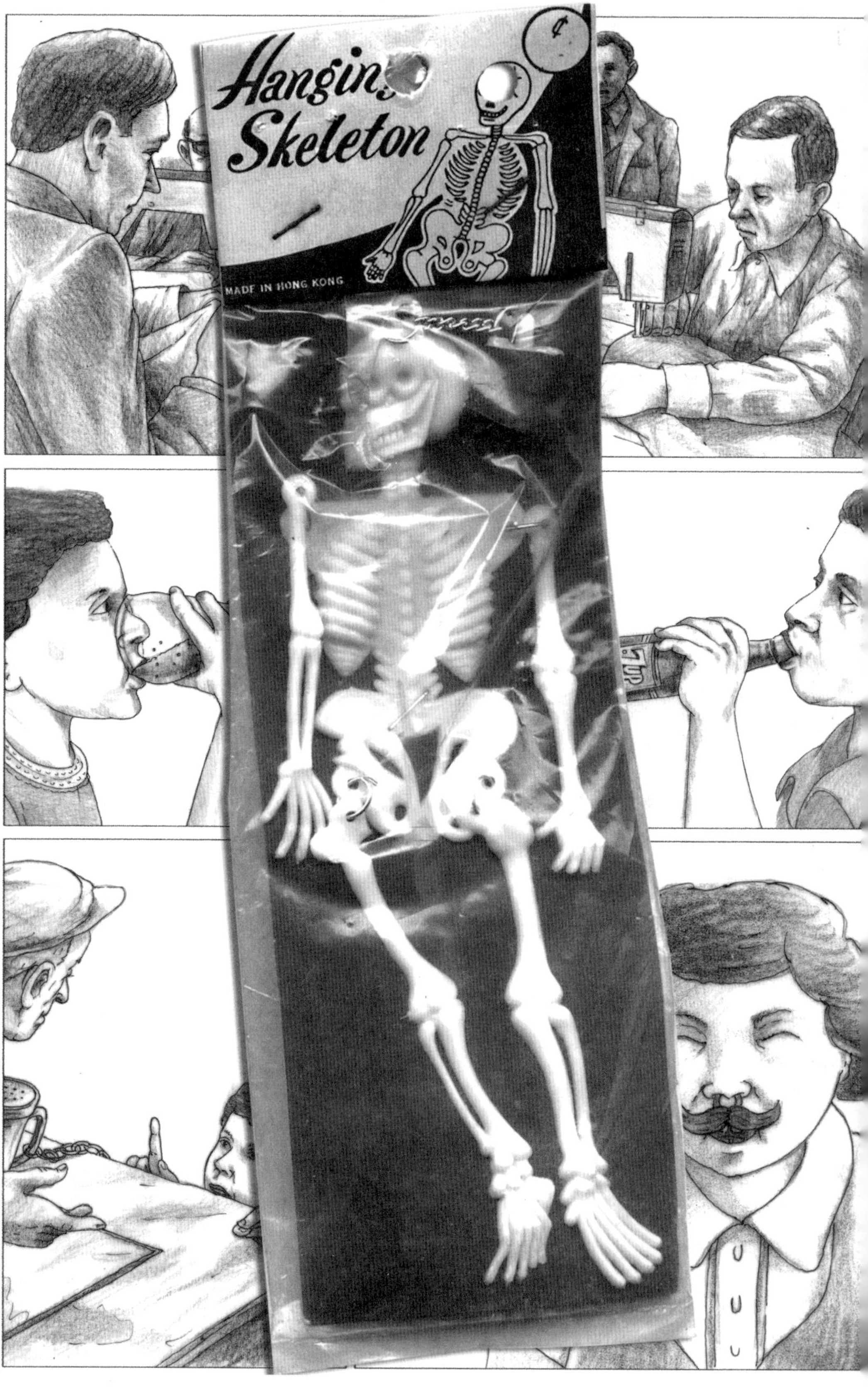
Hangin Skeleton
¢
MADE IN HONG KONG
7Up